Croissant Dozens

Jialin Tian, Ph.D.

Copyright © 2021 by Jialin Tian

Photographs copyright © 2021 by Jialin Tian and Yabin Yu

All rights reserved. No part of this book may be reproduced or transmitted in any form or by any means, electronic or mechanical, including photocopying, recording, or by any information storage and retrieval system, without permission in writing from the publisher.

Disclaimer: While every precaution has been taken in the preparation of this book, the publisher and author assume no responsibility for errors or omissions, or for damage or loss resulting directly or indirectly from the use of the information contained herein.

Published in the United States by Jayca

Photographs and styling: Jialin Tian
Step-by-step photographs and author's photographs: Yabin Yu
Book design and illustrations: Jialin Tian
Production manager: Yabin Yu

www.macaronmagic.com

ISBN 978-1-7334779-1-8

First Edition

INTRODUCTION
6

CROISSANT DOUGH
8

CLASSIC CHARMS

Croissants
20
Pains au Chocolat
24
Raspberry Pains au Chocolat
28
Almond Croissants
30
Peanut Croissants
34
Pepperoni Croissants
36
Chaussons aux Pommes
40
Kouign-Amann
42
Pains Suisses
46

SNAIL FEVER

Pistachio-Raisin Snails
50
Caramel-Walnut Snails
54
Vanilla Snail Muffins
56
Sesame Snail Pairs
60
Strawberry-Chocolate Snails
62
Sfogliatelle
66
Vanilla Double Snails
68
Pizza Snails
72

Fig
Circles
76
Cinnamon Swirls
80
Blueberry Pinwheels
82
Mushroom Turnovers
86
Apricot Diamonds
88

DANISH RETRO

Pistachio-Raspberry Twists
92
Pineapple Squares
94
Maple-Pecan Twists
98
Tropical Diamonds
100
Apricot Pockets
104

Apple
Trees
108
Rose Loaves
112
Meyer Lemon Rolls
114
Hazelnut Sunflowers
118
Cherry-Almond Muffins
120

MODERN CHIC

Espresso-Caramel Loaves
124
Apricot Hearts
126
Mont-Blanc
130
Cassis Knots
132
Whiskey Tarts
136

THEY BELONG IN A ZOO!

Bear Claws
140
Pigs in a Blanket
144
Blueberry Moose
146
Little Pigs in a Blanket
150
Monkey Bread
152
Bacon Monkey Bread
154

INTRODUCTION

Buttery and flaky, delicate and airy, the croissant is a French classic that has been dazzling pastry fans around the globe since it first appeared centuries ago. It was originally an Austrian pastry, and it now occupies its own subcategory in the world of *viennoiseries*, or breads made in the Viennese style. Made by the laminating of yeast-leavened dough, croissants have regained a starring role on the fast-evolving baking scene in recent years.

Croissant Dozens celebrates this baking wonder while showcasing the versatility of croissant dough. Dozens of creations can be derived from one dough, each with its own unique charms but all inheriting the buttery, flaky layers that are the dough's signature characteristic.

In the opening chapter, we introduce the fundamental croissant dough recipe and describe lamination, the principal method for producing the flaky, buttery layers of croissant dough pastries. In the lamination process, a butter block is incorporated into a basic flour dough, and then the dough is rolled out and folded several times to create alternating layers of dough and butter. Here we emphasize clean and precise execution while teaching the valuable tricks of the trade for maximizing a successful outcome.

After the lessons of the dough, we introduce several familiar French classics ranging from the croissant and pain au chocolat to the chausson aux pommes and kouign-amann. Next, we focus on one particular type of rolled and sliced pastry—the snail. You might say we are in a snail fever because we offer eight options, ranging from the familiar pistachio-raisin snail to the sesame snail pair.

Danish settlers brought Viennese-style pastries to America, tempting the American public with rich, layered pastries made with eggs and butter, and the adoring fans responded by calling their beloved pastries "danish." We revisit these irresistible treats by reinventing them with decadent croissant dough accompanied by mouthwatering fillings and toppings. You will see the familiar pinwheels, pockets, swirls, turnovers, and twists with an elegant new look that will entice even the most discerning palates.

In the next chapter, we present ten sophisticated, trendy creations to show off the most modern forms of croissant dough. You will be able to indulge in a beautifully layered croissant loaf filled with a luscious espresso-caramel cream, an exquisite tart containing a rich, whiskey-infused custard, a heart-shaped pastry topped with homemade apricot jam and spiced cookie crumbles, and a reinterpretation of the French classic dessert mont-blanc. You will find it difficult to decide which one of these marvelous creations is your favorite.

In the last chapter, we add whimsy in the form of animal-inspired croissant pastries, from almond-rich bear claws to moose-shaped pastries adorned with jam and chocolate. We offer both sweet and savory options for monkey bread, which uses croissant dough trimmings.

From one croissant dough we have made dozens of extraordinary pastries! Although making the dough is a lengthy process, once you have tried it you will be amazed by the decadent creations you will have. In no time, you will be yearning to make them again! So, without further ado, let's laminate!

CROISSANT DOUGH

In this recipe, we introduce the technique for making croissant dough, which serves as the basis for all the recipes in the rest of the book. A well-made croissant dough pastry possesses the characteristics of a flaky exterior, a delicate and moist interior, and a buttery and yeasty aroma. Croissant dough can be viewed as a hybrid product between a puff pastry and a bread dough, and both of these doughs contribute to the croissant's airiness. These two sources of lift are generated from lamination and fermentation. In the lamination process, a butter block is first encased in floury dough, and then the dough is rolled out and folded several times to create alternating layers of dough and butter. During baking, the water in the butter evaporates and forms steam, which is responsible for creating the flaky, airy layers. In addition to lamination, during fermentation, yeast consumes sugars and starches in the dough and produces carbon dioxide and alcohol. During baking, fermentation creates both the lift and the signature yeasty aroma of a croissant pastry.

In the recipes in this book, we perform the lamination process by hand instead of using a sheeter, as is widely done by professional bakers. Lamination by hand can be challenging, but with special attention to details and meticulous execution, you can produce professional-quality croissant dough using just a rolling pin.

Note: This recipe employs a 3-day fermentation process. Although it is a relatively lengthy process, the use of a starter and long cold fermentation period is well worth the effort. The resulting pastries are much crunchier, with complex and delicate flavors.

Note: In this recipe, we use equal amounts of bread flour and all-purpose flour. The high-protein bread flour gives the final product the desired structure, and the all-purpose flour helps to produce a delicate texture. The butter in the dough also helps to produce fine, tender crumbs. In addition, the amount of all-purpose flour and butter in the dough makes rolling by hand much easier.

Yield: about 2.3 kg/5 lb dough

INGREDIENTS

Starter:

100 g/3.5 oz bread flour

100 g/3.5 oz water, at room temperature

Dough:

30 g/1.1 oz active dry yeast (reduce to 25 g/0.88 oz during summer months)

280 g/10 oz water, at room temperature

150 g/5.3 oz whole milk, cold

1 egg (about 50 g/1.8 oz)

130 g/4.6 oz granulated sugar

20 g/0.71 oz kosher salt

500 g/1.1 lb bread flour

500 g/1.1 lb all-purpose flour

225 g/8 oz unsalted butter (82% butterfat), at room temperature

Butter for Lamination:

450 g/1 lb unsalted butter (82% butterfat), at room temperature

Day 1

To make the starter:

Combine the bread flour and water in a mixing bowl. Mix all the ingredients into a paste.

Cover the bowl with plastic wrap and let it rest overnight at room temperature.

Day 2

To make the dough:

Mix the active dry yeast with water in a stand mixer bowl [1]. Use a spoon to stir the mixture until all of the yeast is dissolved.

Add the cold milk, egg, sugar, and salt into the mixer bowl. Mix to combine using a whisk. Add the bread flour, all-purpose flour, softened butter, and starter mixture from the previous day [2].

Attach the bowl to a stand mixer fitted with a dough hook attachment. Knead the dough on low speed for about 10 to 15 minutes until the dough comes together [3, 4].

Take the dough out of the bowl and knead it by hand for 2 to 3 minutes [5]. Shape the dough into a smooth ball [6]. Place the dough ball back into the mixer bowl. Cover it with plastic wrap, and let it rise at room temperature for about 30 to 40 minutes.

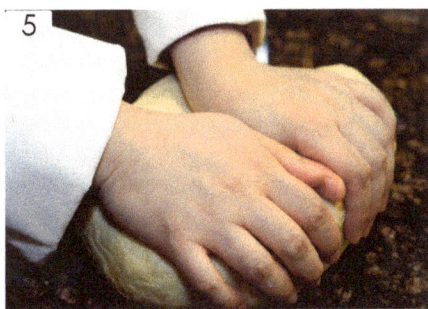

After the first rise, place the dough ball on a lightly floured work surface with the smooth side up. Cut a cross into the top of the dough [7, 8]. Push the four tips of the cross outward to shape the dough into a square [9, 10]. Use a rolling pin to roll the dough into a 43-cm x 30-cm/17-in x 12-in rectangle [11].

Transfer the dough onto a half-sheet baking pan lined with parchment paper [12]. Press the dough slightly until it has a snug fit against the edges of the baking pan [13, 14]. Cover the dough with another piece of parchment paper, and place plastic wrap on top of that. Let the dough ferment in the refrigerator overnight.

Note: On average, one batch of the recipe produces approximately 27 individual pastries. The relatively large quantity has four advantages. First of all, the 3-day fermentation and lamination efforts are necessary regardless of the batch size; therefore, making a large batch is much more labor effective than making several small batches. Second, during lamination the uneven edges are trimmed off; therefore, a large batch offers a much higher ratio of useable dough to trimmings. Third, croissant dough and its finished pastry products freeze well, so pastries that will not be eaten right away can be frozen and enjoyed later. Finally, each of the pastries in this book calls for one third of the croissant dough in the basic recipe; therefore, you can make three different croissant creations from one batch of dough and have them ready for a beautiful breakfast buffet.

Note: The quality and consistency of the butter used in croissant dough is crucial. Use only high-quality European-style butter that is low in water content and high in fat content (with at least 82% of butterfat). In addition, the temperature of the butter is vital to ensure the success of the outcome. If the butter block is too cold when it is incorporated into the floury dough, butter patches will form during rolling, and this will cause excess butter to ooze out during baking. On the other hand, if the butter is too warm, it will melt during rolling, and the desired layering effect will be lost.

To prepare the butter for lamination:

Place the softened butter between two pieces of parchment paper. Use a rolling pin to flatten the butter slightly [15].

Fold the parchment paper around the butter to form a 24-cm x 30-cm/9.4-in x 12-in rectangle [16]. Roll the butter into an even layer that fits the rectangular shape [17, 18]. Refrigerate the butter block.

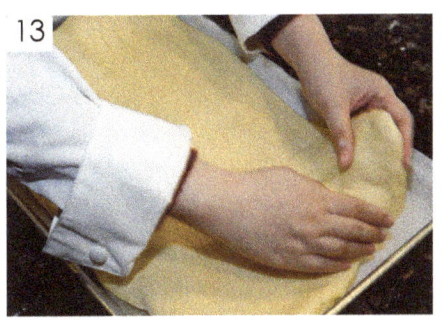

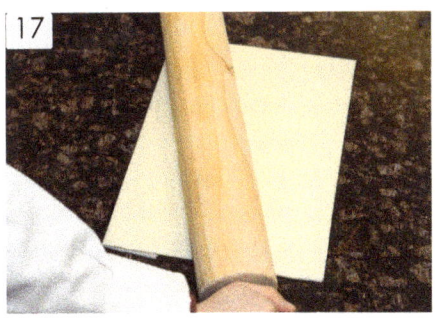

CROISSANT DOUGH

Day 3

To laminate the dough:

Take the butter for lamination out of the refrigerator. Peel back the parchment paper [19]. Leave the butter on the parchment paper until it warms up slightly [20]. Let the butter sit at room temperature for about 20 to 30 minutes so that it is still cold but is also pliable (about 13°C/55°F to 16°C/60°F).

Take the dough out of the refrigerator. Peel off and discard the parchment paper. Place the dough on a lightly floured work surface, and use a rolling pin to roll it out to a 50-cm x 30-cm/20-in x 12-in rectangle [21].

Note: The lamination process is accomplished by sequential steps of rolling and folding of the butter-encased dough. There are four popular lamination configurations: two single turns (or letter folds) producing nine layers of butter, one single turn plus one double turn (or book folds) producing twelve layers of butter, two double turns producing sixteen layers of butter, and three single turns producing twenty-seven layers of butter. The method using two single turns creates a coarse texture of the final product, whereas the method using three single turns risks having the layers merge together indistinguishably. The method using one single turn plus one double turn and the method using two double turns are both more suitable candidates. Because rolling by hand produces a thicker dough than industrial sheeting (which produces a standard thickness of 3-mm/0.12-in to 4-mm/0.16-in), the hand-rolled dough can accommodate more layers. We have chosen the method using two double turns in this book.

Note: If the dough is thick to start with, it helps to pound it out into a thin dough and then start to roll. If the amount of dough is large, I recommend using a long rolling pin, such as my 46-cm/18-in maple wood rolling pin. In addition, it is helpful to change the rolling angles and directions, for example, rolling on a diagonal to extend the height of the dough. If the dough sticks to the surface, lift up the dough and dust more flour underneath it.

Note: At each stage, we score the folding edges to help the butter extend to the edges while rolling. Also, we trim off the uneven edges after rolling out the dough. These steps help to create even layers, and this is essential for creating the desired lamination.

Using the parchment paper that is holding the butter, invert the butter onto the center of the dough [22]. The shorter edge of the butter block aligns with the longer edge of the dough. Fold the left and right sides of the dough to encase the butter [23, 24]. Use a knife to lightly score both the left and right folding edges [25, 26].

On a lightly floured surface, roll the dough out to a 90-cm x 38-cm/35-in x 15-in rectangle [27, 28]. Trim off any uneven edges from both the left and right sides [29, 30].

CROISSANT DOUGH   13

With the seam side up, give the dough a double turn (book folds). This can be done by first folding the left edge to the right about halfway [31] and then folding the right edge to the left to meet the left edge in the middle [32]. Score the folding edges on both sides [33, 34]. Finally, fold the left side to the right as if you are closing a book [35]. Score the folding edge again [36]. Place the dough on a sheet pan [37]. Cover the dough with plastic wrap, and let it rest for 30 minutes in the refrigerator.

Roll the dough out again to a 90-cm x 38-cm/35-in x 15-in rectangle. Trim off any uneven edges from both the left and right sides. Save the trimmings for another use. Give the dough another double turn. Be sure to score the folding edges. Cover the dough with plastic wrap, and let it rest for 30 minutes in the refrigerator.

Note: Commercial bakers use sheeters or laminators to roll out the dough into thin, even dough sheets. Lamination by hand using a rolling pin can be intimidating, but it is achievable if care is taken. The winter months are ideal for making croissant dough because the indoor temperature is around 21°C/70°F. A sturdy hard surface is required for rolling out the dough. During warmer months, when the indoor temperature is above 24°C/75°F, it is important to work rapidly. If the butter starts to melt, fold up the dough and return it to the refrigerator until it is cold enough to work with again.

Note: Croissant dough and its final products are ideal for freezing at different stages. The laminated dough can be portioned, wrapped, and frozen. When you are ready to use the dough, defrost it in the refrigerator overnight. Shaped, unbaked croissant pastries can be frozen, as well. Simply defrost and proof the shaped pastries at room temperature for 3 to 4 hours before baking. In addition, baked croissant pastries can be frozen. You can defrost the frozen baked pastries in the refrigerator for a few hours and then heat them up in a 177°C/350°F oven for about 10 to 15 minutes.

Roll the dough out to a 60-cm x 30-cm/24-in x 12-in rectangle [38]. Cut the dough into three equal portions [39-41]. Each portion will be 20-cm x 30-cm/8-in x 12-in, and each piece will weigh about 760 g/1.7 lb. Let the dough rest for 30 minutes in the refrigerator. The dough is ready to use. Recipes in this book call for one of the three portions [42].

CROISSANT DOUGH

CROISSANT DOUGH LAMINATION QUICK REFERENCE

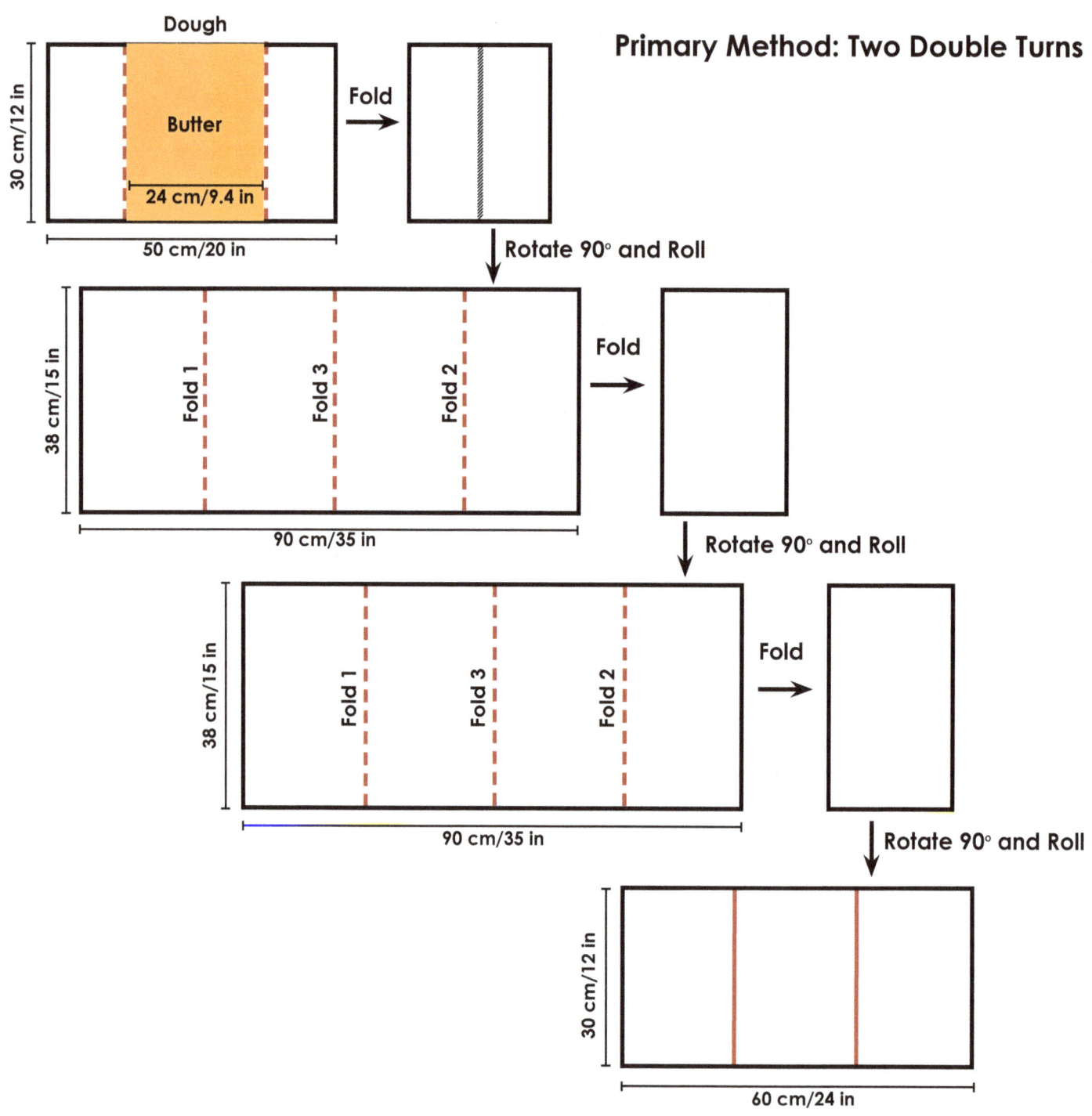

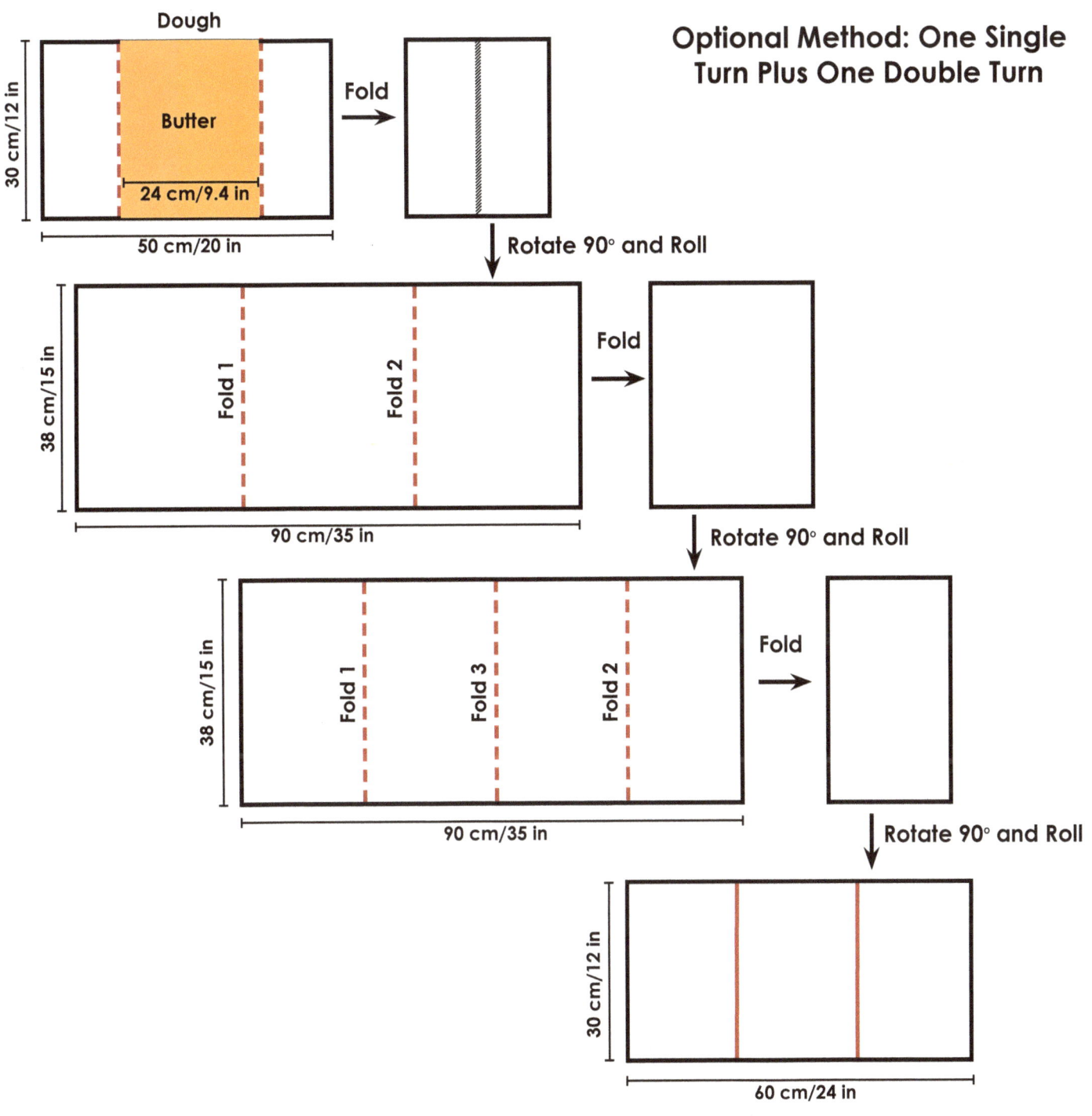

CROISSANT DOUGH 17

CLASSIC CHARMS

CROISSANTS

Perhaps the best-known French pastry creation, croissants have been dazzling pastry fans around the globe for centuries. The croissant has its own subcategory in the world of *viennoiseries*, or breads made in the Viennese style. Croissants originated in Austria centuries ago, and modern croissants have been perfected by French bakers since then. Although various methods exist for producing croissants, the lamination technique with yeast-leavened dough produces the most prestigious and authentic croissants, or classic butter croissants. A well-made croissant should have a flaky, caramelized exterior and a delicate and airy interior, and it should be full of a buttery, nutty, fermented flavor.

Yield: 9 regular croissants or 7 big croissants

INGREDIENTS

760 g/1.7 lb croissant dough (page 8)

1 egg

10 g/0.35 oz (2 tsp) heavy cream

Follow the recipe on page 8 to make a croissant dough. Take one of three portions of the dough (weighs about 760 g/1.7 lb).

Roll out the croissant dough into a rectangle that is slightly larger than 40-cm x 28-cm/16-in x 11-in in size [1]. Trim off the uneven edges [2].

Note: To make 7 big croissants, roll the dough into a rectangle that is slightly larger than 32-cm x 28-cm/13-in x 11-in in size.

Use a knife to mark the dough at 8-cm/3.1-in intervals on the bottom edge [3]. Begin with a 4-cm/1.6-in offset, and mark the dough at 8-cm/3.1-in intervals on the top edge.

Place a ruler on a diagonal line according to the marks, and cut out a triangular piece that is 8-cm/3.1-in wide at the base and 28-cm/11-in in height. Repeat to cut out the remaining pieces [4, 5].

Take a piece of the dough, and cut a 2.5-cm/1-in slit in the middle at the base of the dough [6]. Using two fingers, fold the two tips upward, and then apply gentle pressure to roll up the piece to form the croissant shape [7-10]. Finish shaping the remaining pieces [11].

Place the shaped croissants on a baking pan lined with parchment paper while leaving ample space among the pieces [12]. Cover with plastic wrap, and allow the pieces to proof for 1.5 to 2.5 hours or until doubled in volume at room temperature [13].

Meanwhile, preheat the oven to 188°C/370°F.

In a bowl, whisk the egg with the heavy cream. Brush the croissants gently with the egg wash [14]. Take care not to cover the layers with egg wash.

Bake the croissants for about 20 to 25 minutes until they are golden brown [15, 16]. Add 5 more minutes of baking time for big croissants. Let the croissants cool slightly before serving.

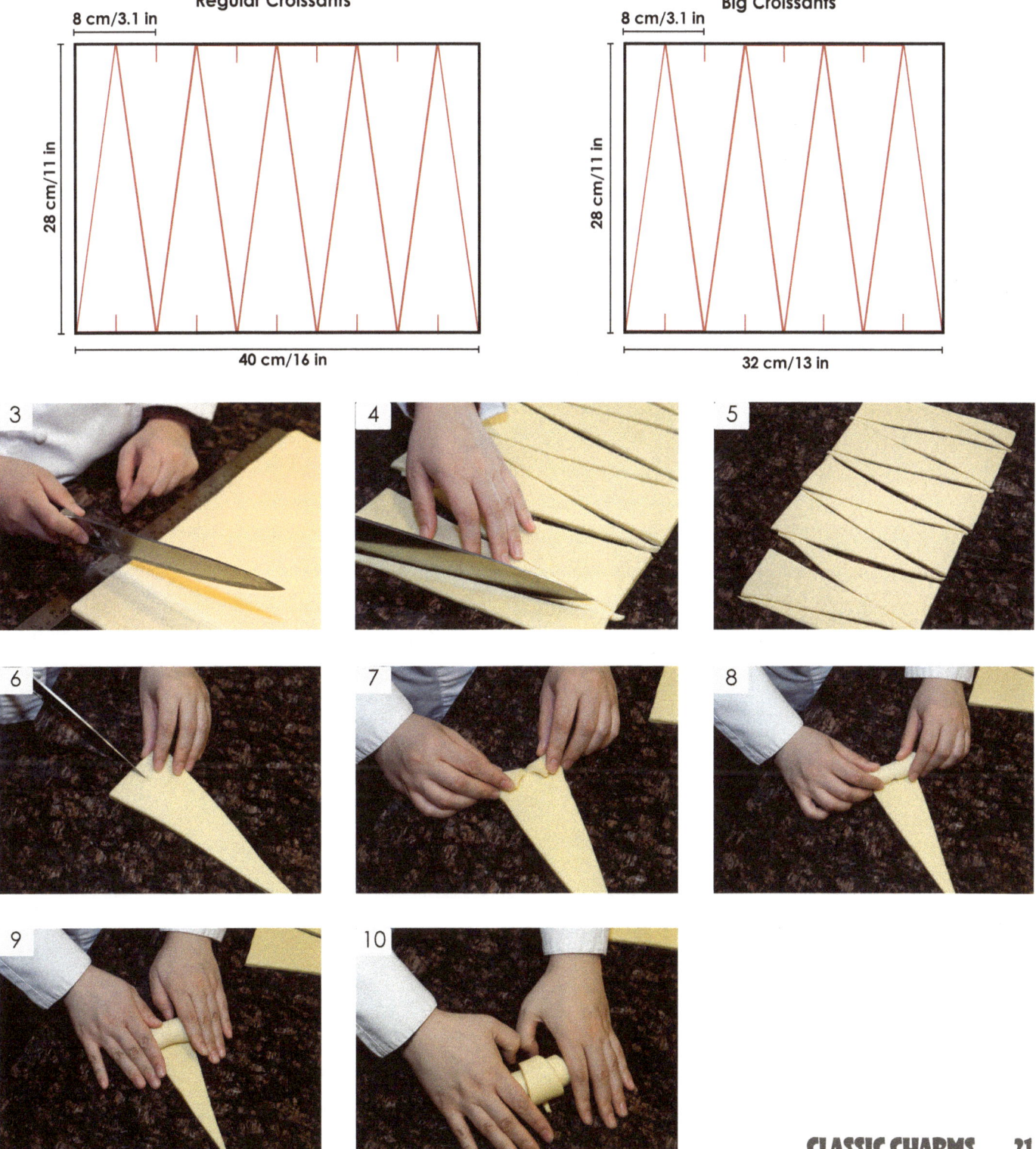

PAINS AU CHOCOLAT

Chances are wherever you see croissants, you will find pains au chocolat, or chocolate bread. Sometimes it is known as the chocolate croissant. Pain au chocolat is made from buttery, flaky croissant dough wrapped around two dark chocolate sticks and rolled up to a shape like a pillow. This crackly croissant variation is absolutely brilliant! The chocolate sticks are especially designed for making pains au chocolat. You can substitute chocolate chips for the chocolate sticks if you don't have the sticks on hand.

Yield: 9 individual pastries

INGREDIENTS

760 g/1.7 lb croissant dough (page 8)

18 chocolate sticks

1 egg

10 g/0.35 oz (2 tsp) heavy cream

Follow the recipe on page 8 to make a croissant dough. Take one of three portions of the dough (weighs about 760 g/1.7 lb).

Roll out the croissant dough into a rectangle that is slightly larger than 24-cm x 48-cm/9.4-in x 19-in in size [1]. Trim off the uneven edges [2].

Use a knife to cut the dough into three strips [3], each the size of 24-cm x 16-cm/9.4-in x 6.3-in. Cut each strip into three pieces [4, 5], each the size of 8-cm x 16-cm/3.1-in x 6.3-in. There will be a total of nine dough pieces.

Take a piece of the dough and facing the shorter edge, place a chocolate stick at the bottom horizontally and roll up the dough to cover the chocolate stick [6]. Place a second chocolate stick on the dough horizontally [7]. Finish rolling up the dough piece [8, 9]. Repeat to finish shaping the remaining dough pieces [10].

Place the shaped pastries on a baking pan lined with parchment paper while leaving ample space among the pieces. Cover with plastic wrap, and allow the pieces to proof for 1.5 to 2.5 hours or until doubled in volume at room temperature [11].

Meanwhile, preheat the oven to 188°C/370°F.

In a bowl, whisk the egg with the heavy cream. Brush the pastries gently with the egg wash [12]. Take care not to cover the layers with egg wash.

Bake the pastries for about 20 to 25 minutes until they are golden brown [13, 14]. Let them cool slightly before serving.

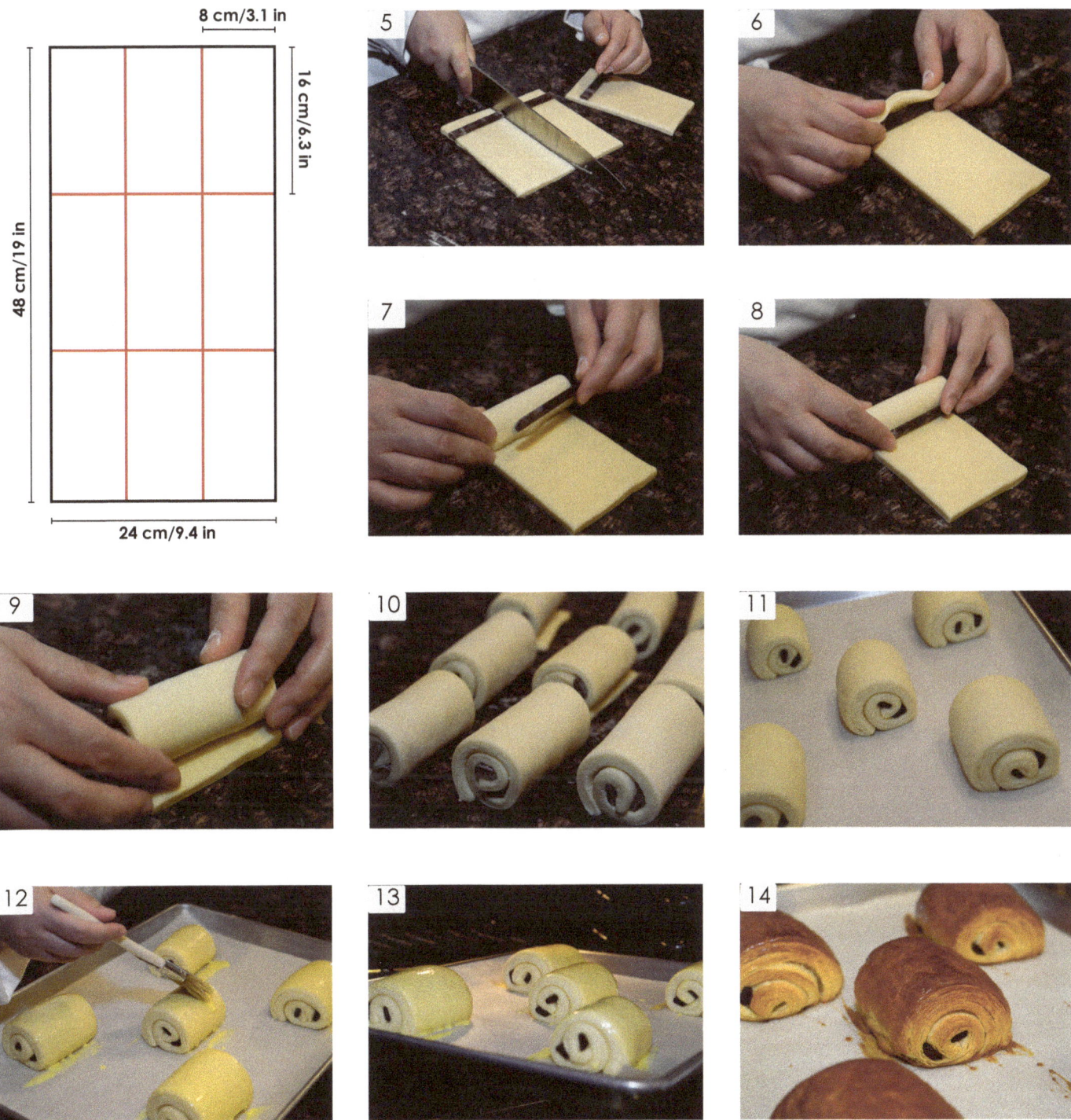

CLASSIC CHARMS 25

PAINS AU CHOCOLAT

RASPBERRY PAINS AU CHOCOLAT

RASPBERRY PAINS AU CHOCOLAT

This variation of the pain au chocolat incorporates homemade raspberry jam as well as chocolate into the pastry. When you bite into it, you discover warm, flaky layers of pastry with intense dark chocolate mingled with sweet, fruity raspberry jam in the center. It is truly a delectable variation of the classic.

Yield: 9 individual pastries

INGREDIENTS

760 g/1.7 lb croissant dough (page 8)

Raspberry Jam:

80 g/2.8 oz granulated sugar

2 g/0.071 oz (½ tsp) powdered pectin

170 g/6 oz raspberry puree

Baking Finishes:

18 chocolate sticks

1 egg

10 g/0.35 oz (2 tsp) heavy cream

Follow the recipe on page 8 to make a croissant dough. Take one of three portions of the dough (weighs about 760 g/1.7 lb) and cover it with plastic wrap. Reserve the dough in the refrigerator until you are ready to use it.

Raspberry Jam:

Combine half of the sugar (40 g/1.4 oz) and the pectin in a mixing bowl. Mix thoroughly and reserve.

In a medium-sized saucepan, combine the raspberry puree with the remaining sugar (40 g/1.4 oz). Bring the mixture to a boil over medium-high heat. Stir in the sugar-pectin mixture [1]. Bring the mixture back to a boil and reduce the heat to medium-low. Stir constantly and cook for another 5 minutes [2]. Let the mixture cool slightly. Cover the surface of the jam with plastic wrap and store it in the refrigerator until you are ready to use it.

Shaping and Baking:

Roll out the croissant dough into a rectangle that is slightly larger than 24-cm x 48-cm/9.4-in x 19-in in size. Trim off the uneven edges.

Use a knife to cut the dough into three strips, each the size of 24-cm x 16-cm/9.4-in x 6.3-in. Cut each strip into three pieces [3], each the size of 8-cm x 16-cm/3.1-in x 6.3-in. There will be a total of nine dough pieces.

To make a design on the dough, freeze the dough pieces for 5 to 10 minutes. Take one piece of the dough and use a paring knife to score half of the dough piece [4]. Repeat to finish making the design for the remaining dough pieces.

Turn over a piece of the dough and make sure the design will show on top after the piece is folded. If the dough is still too hard to be shaped, wait a few minutes.

Facing the shorter edge, spread a small amount of the raspberry jam on top of the dough using a small offset spatula [5]. Place a chocolate stick at the bottom horizontally and roll up the dough to cover the chocolate stick [6]. Place a second chocolate stick on the dough horizontally [7]. Finish rolling up the dough piece. Repeat to finish shaping the remaining dough pieces.

Place the shaped pastries on a baking pan lined with parchment paper while leaving ample space among the pieces [8]. Cover with plastic wrap and allow the pieces to proof for 1.5 to 2.5 hours or until doubled in volume at room temperature.

Meanwhile, preheat the oven to 188°C/370°F. In a bowl, whisk the egg with the heavy cream. Brush the pastries gently with the egg wash [9]. Take care not to cover the layers with egg wash. Bake the pastries for about 20 to 25 minutes until they are golden brown [10, 11]. Let them cool slightly before serving.

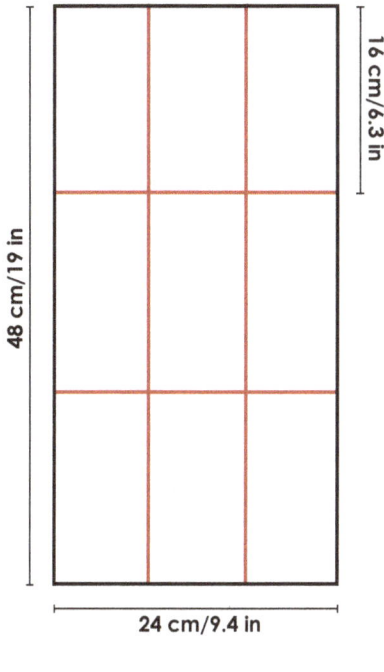

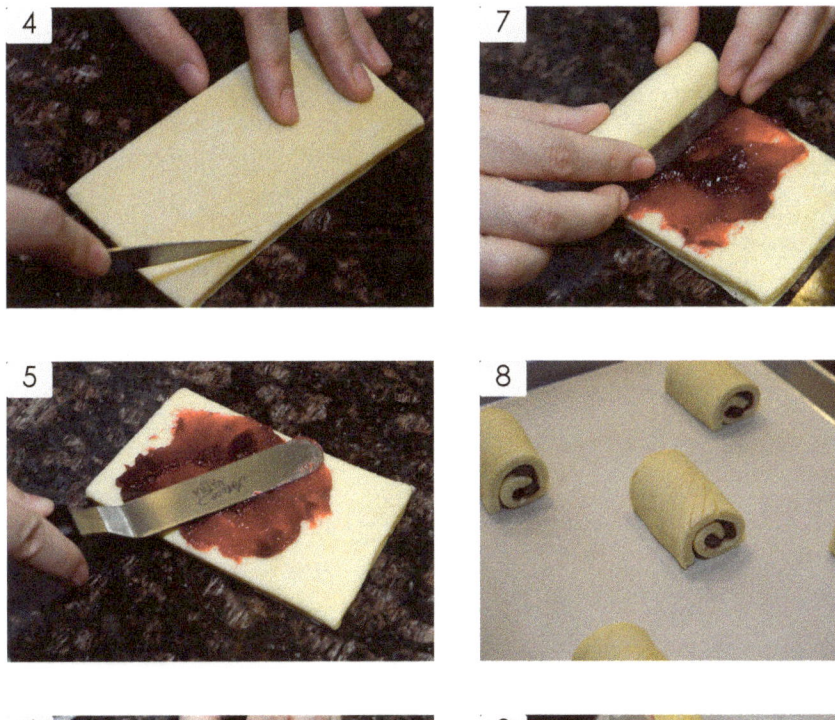

CLASSIC CHARMS

ALMOND CROISSANTS

The almond croissant is another French bakery classic. Normally, bakers use leftover stale croissants by filling them with almond-based frangipane cream and then bake them for a second time. This version of the almond croissant uses fresh croissant dough and is baked with almond filling only once. A drop of rose essence elevates this exquisite pastry to a whole new level. It is shaped like the pain au chocolat rather than the croissant to minimize leakage during baking.

Yield: 9 individual pastries

INGREDIENTS

760 g/1.7 lb croissant dough (page 8)

Almond-Rose Filling:

100 g/3.5 oz almond paste

50 g/1.8 oz unsalted butter, at room temperature

1 egg white (about 30 g/1.1 oz)

5 g/0.18 oz (1 tsp) rose extract

50 g/1.8 oz almond slices

Baking Finishes:

1 egg

10 g/0.35 oz (2 tsp) heavy cream

Almond slices

Powdered sugar for dusting

Follow the recipe on page 8 to make a croissant dough. Take one of three portions of the dough (weighs about 760 g/1.7 lb) and cover it with plastic wrap. Reserve the dough in the refrigerator until you are ready to use it.

Almond-Rose Filling:

In a mixing bowl, combine the almond paste, butter, egg white, and rose extract. Mix all the ingredients into a paste using a spoon.

Add the almond slices to the mixture. Mix well. Cover the bowl with plastic wrap. Store the filling in the refrigerator if you are not using it immediately. Use it at room temperature.

Shaping and Baking:

Roll out the croissant dough into a rectangle that is slightly larger than 24-cm x 48-cm/9.4-in x 19-in in size [1]. Trim off the uneven edges.

Spread the almond-rose filling on top of the dough using an offset spatula [2].

Use a knife to cut the dough into three strips, each the size of 24-cm x 16-cm/9.4-in x 6.3-in. Cut each strip into three pieces, each the size of 8-cm x 16-cm/3.1-in x 6.3-in. There will be a total of nine dough pieces [3].

Take a piece of the dough and facing the shorter edge, roll up the dough [4, 5]. Repeat to finish shaping the remaining dough pieces.

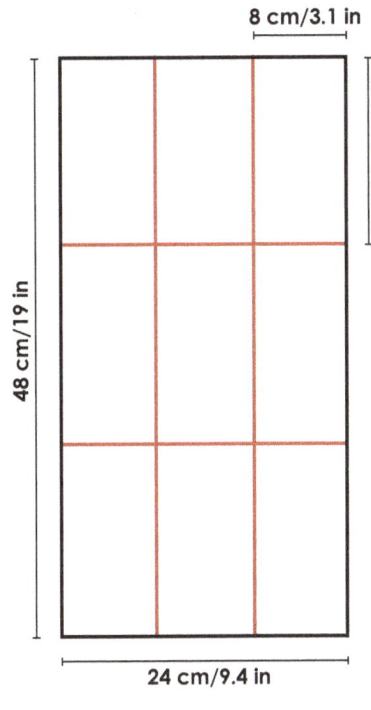

Place the shaped pastries on a baking pan lined with parchment paper while leaving ample space among the pieces [6]. Cover with plastic wrap and allow the pieces to proof for 1.5 to 2.5 hours or until doubled in volume at room temperature.

Meanwhile, preheat the oven to 188°C/370°F.

In a bowl, whisk the egg with the heavy cream. Brush the pastries gently with the egg wash [7]. Take care not to cover the layers with egg wash. Sprinkle almond slices on top of each pastry [8].

Bake the pastries for about 20 to 25 minutes until they are golden brown [9]. Dust the pastries with powdered sugar [10]. Let them cool slightly before serving.

CLASSIC CHARMS

ALMOND CROISSANTS

PEANUT CROISSANTS

In this variation of the classic croissant, you will find flaky, buttery layers of pastry filled with almond-peanut paste in the center. It's an absolutely delightful nutty alternative.

Yield: 8 individual pastries

INGREDIENTS

760 g/1.7 lb croissant dough (page 8)

Peanut Filling:

120 g/4.2 oz almond paste

30 g/1.1 oz peanut butter

30 g/1.1 oz roasted peanuts, chopped

Baking Finishes:

1 egg

10 g/0.35 oz (2 tsp) heavy cream

Chopped peanuts

Follow the recipe on page 8 to make a croissant dough. Take one of three portions of the dough (weighs about 760 g/1.7 lb) and cover it with plastic wrap. Reserve the dough in the refrigerator until you are ready to use it.

Peanut Filling:

In a mixing bowl, combine the almond paste and the peanut butter. Mix well using a spoon. Stir in the chopped peanuts. Cover the bowl with plastic wrap. Reserve in the refrigerator until you are ready to use it.

Shaping and Baking:

Roll out the croissant dough into a rectangle that is slightly larger than 36-cm x 28-cm/14-in x 11-in in size. Trim off the uneven edges.

Use a knife to mark the dough at 8-cm/3.1-in intervals on the bottom edge. Begin with a 4-cm/1.6-in offset, and mark the dough at 8-cm/3.1-in intervals on the top edge.

Place a ruler on a diagonal line according to the marks, and cut out a triangular piece that is 8-cm/3.1-in wide at the base and 28-cm/11-in in height. Repeat to cut out the remaining pieces [1].

Take a piece of the dough and cut a 2.5-cm/1-in slit in the middle at the base of the dough [2]. Take a spoonful of the peanut filling and shape it into a 6-cm/2.4-in log. Place the log at the base of the dough piece [3]. Using two fingers, fold the two tips upward, and then apply gentle pressure to roll up the piece to form the croissant shape [4-6]. Finish shaping the remaining pieces.

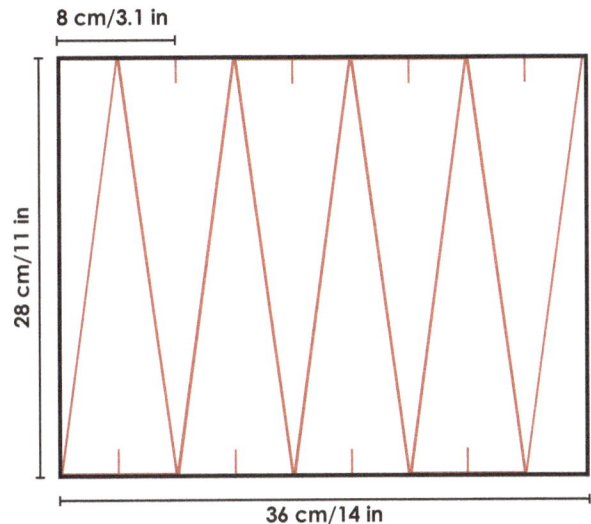

Place the shaped croissants on a baking pan lined with parchment paper while leaving ample space among the pieces [7]. Cover with plastic wrap, and allow the pieces to proof for 1.5 to 2.5 hours or until doubled in volume at room temperature.

Meanwhile, preheat the oven to 188°C/370°F. In a bowl, whisk the egg with the heavy cream. Brush the croissants gently with the egg wash [8]. Take care not to cover the layers with egg wash. Sprinkle the croissants with the chopped peanuts [9].

Bake the croissants for about 20 to 25 minutes until they are golden brown [10, 11]. Let them cool slightly before serving.

CLASSIC CHARMS

PEPPERONI CROISSANTS

This savory croissant is filled with melty mozzarella and flavorful pepperoni. It's perfect for a light lunch or snack on the go.

Yield: 8 individual pastries

INGREDIENTS

760 g/1.7 lb croissant dough (page 8)

180 g/6.3 oz mozzarella cheese

100 g/3.5 oz pepperoni slices

1 egg

10 g/0.35 oz (2 tsp) heavy cream

Follow the recipe on page 8 to make a croissant dough. Take one of three portions of the dough (weighs about 760 g/1.7 lb).

Cut the mozzarella cheese into sticks 7-cm/2.8-in long. Set them aside.

Roll out the croissant dough into a rectangle that is slightly larger than 36-cm x 28-cm/14-in x 11-in in size. Trim off the uneven edges.

Use a knife to mark the dough at 8-cm/3.1-in intervals on the bottom edge. Begin with a 4-cm/1.6-in offset and mark the dough at 8-cm/3.1-in intervals on the top edge.

Place a ruler on a diagonal line according to the marks, and cut out a triangular piece that is 8-cm/3.1-in wide at the base and 28-cm/11-in in height. Repeat to cut out the remaining pieces [1].

Take a piece of the dough and cut a 2.5-cm/1-in slit in the middle at the base of the dough [2]. Place a few slices of pepperoni and one mozzarella stick at the base of the dough piece [3, 4]. Using two fingers, fold the two tips upward, and then apply gentle pressure to roll up the piece to form the croissant shape [5-7]. Finish shaping the remaining pieces [8].

Place the shaped croissants on a baking pan lined with parchment paper while leaving ample space among the pieces [9]. Cover with plastic wrap, and allow the pieces to proof for 1.5 to 2.5 hours or until doubled in volume at room temperature.

Meanwhile, preheat the oven to 188°C/370°F. In a bowl, whisk the egg with the heavy cream. Brush the croissants gently with the egg wash [10]. Take care not to cover the layers with egg wash. Bake the croissants for about 20 to 25 minutes until they are golden brown [11]. Let them cool slightly before serving.

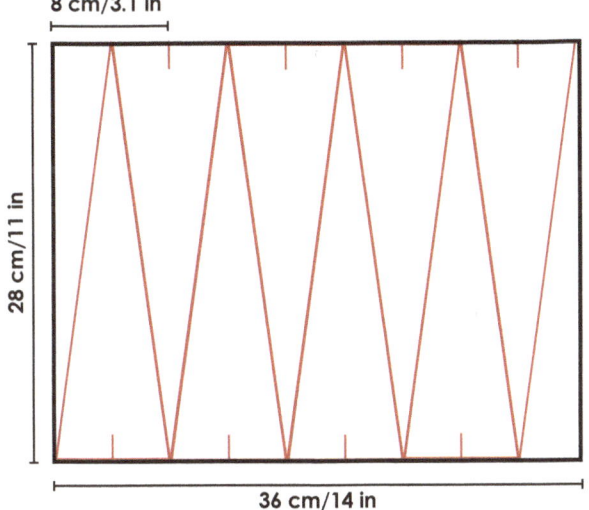

CLASSIC CHARMS

PEPPERONI CROISSANTS

CHAUSSONS AUX POMMES

CHAUSSONS AUX POMMES

The chausson aux pommes, or apple turnover, is a familiar item in the French bakery repertoire. Traditionally, apple turnovers are made with puff pastry dough, but this version is made with croissant dough. Not only does it possess the signature flaky layers but it also has the tantalizing aroma of bread. The addition of calvados (aged apple brandy) and raisins further intensifies the apple flavor and enhances the texture of the apple compote. It is a delightful reinterpretation of a timeless classic.

Yield: 6 individual pastries

Ingredients

760 g/1.7 lb croissant dough (page 8)

Caramel-Apple Compote:

40 g/1.4 oz heavy cream

80 g/2.8 oz granulated sugar

400 g/14 oz Granny Smith apple cubes

15 g/0.53 oz calvados (aged apple brandy)

80 g/2.8 oz raisins

Baking Finishes:

1 egg

10 g/0.35 oz (2 tsp) heavy cream

Follow the recipe on page 8 to make a croissant dough. Take one of three portions of the dough (weighs about 760 g/1.7 lb) and cover it with plastic wrap. Reserve the dough in the refrigerator until you are ready to use it.

Caramel-Apple Compote:

To make the caramel, place the heavy cream in a medium-sized saucepan. Heat the cream over high heat. Remove the pan from the heat when the cream comes to a boil. Reserve.

Place the sugar in a large saucepan in an even layer. Dry melt the sugar over medium heat undisturbed for 2 to 4 minutes. When most of the sugar underneath the top layer of granules is melted and has turned a golden color, reduce the heat to low. Stir occasionally with a spatula to avoid burning the caramel.

When all of the sugar is melted and the caramel turns a medium-dark amber color, pour the reserved hot cream into the pan [1]. Stir it vigorously to smooth out any lumps.

Add the apple cubes to the pan [2]. Continue to cook the apples for another 8 to 10 minutes while stirring constantly. Add the calvados to deglaze the pan, and then add the raisins to the pan. Stir to combine [3].

Transfer the caramel-apple compote to a bowl and let it cool. Cover the bowl with plastic wrap and store the compote in the refrigerator until you are ready to use it.

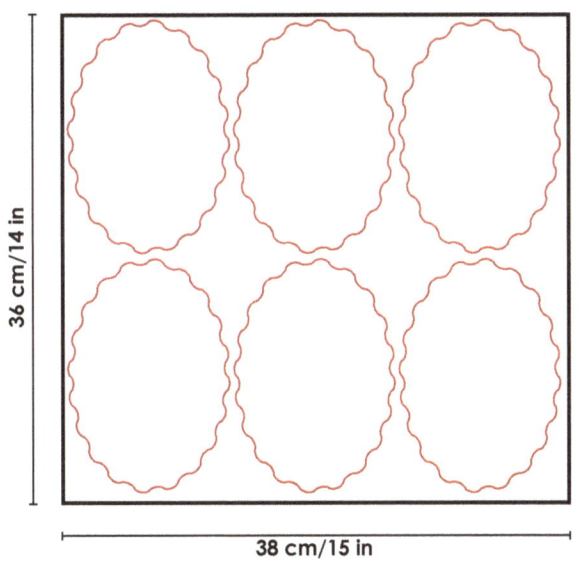

Shaping and Baking:

Roll out the croissant dough to about 38-cm x 36-cm/15-in x 14-in in size. Use a 12-cm x 17-cm/4.7-in x 6.7-in oval cutter to cut out six pieces of the dough [4].

To make a design on the dough, freeze the dough pieces for 5 to 10 minutes. Take one piece of the dough and use a paring knife to score half of the dough piece [5]. Repeat to make the design for the remaining dough pieces.

Turn over a piece of the dough and make sure the design will show on top after the piece is folded. If the dough is still too hard to be shaped, wait a few minutes. Place a spoonful of the caramel-apple filling on top of the dough. Brush the edge with water [6]. Fold the piece in half to enclose the filling. Press the edge to seal the turnover [7]. Repeat to finish forming the remaining dough pieces.

Place the shaped pastries on a baking pan lined with parchment paper while leaving ample space among the pieces. Cover with plastic wrap, and allow the pieces to proof for 1.5 to 2.5 hours or until doubled in volume at room temperature.

Meanwhile, preheat the oven to 188°C/370°F. In a bowl, whisk the egg with the heavy cream. Brush the pastries gently with the egg wash [8]. Take care not to cover the layers with egg wash. Bake the pastries for about 25 to 30 minutes until they are golden brown [9]. Let them cool slightly before serving.

CLASSIC CHARMS

KOUIGN-AMANN

An exquisite specialty of Brittany, kouign-amann pastries are made from croissant dough that has been laminated with sugar and butter. This results in flaky croissant layers covered with crunchy, sweet caramelized sugar. It's the ultimate indulgence. This version of the pastry offers a reduced-calorie alternative in which the croissant dough is laminated with only butter and then coated with sugar. The crunchy caramel on the bottom and crystalized sugar on top produce a delightful textural synchronization.

Yield: 9 individual pastries

Ingredients

760 g/1.7 lb croissant dough (page 8)

160 g/5.6 oz granulated sugar

Follow the recipe on page 8 to make a croissant dough. Take one of three portions of the dough (weighs about 760 g/1.7 lb).

Roll out the croissant dough into a square that is slightly larger than 30-cm x 30-cm/12-in x 12-in in size. Trim off the uneven edges. Cut the dough into nine squares, each 10-cm x 10-cm/4-in x 4-in.

Place the sugar on a plate. Butter nine ring molds that are 9-cm/3.5-in in diameter (5-cm/2-in in height) [1]. Coat the inside of each buttered mold with sugar [2]. Place the molds on top of a baking pan lined with parchment paper. Sprinkle more sugar at the bottom of each mold [3].

Take one piece of the dough and press the dough into the sugar [4]. Turn the piece over to coat the other side with more sugar [5].

Fold the four corners of the sugar-coated dough piece toward the center [6]. Place the shaped pastry inside a ring mold. Repeat to finish shaping the remaining pieces [7]. Reserve any leftover sugar.

Cover with plastic wrap, and allow the pieces to proof for 1.5 to 2.5 hours or until doubled in volume at room temperature.

Meanwhile, preheat the oven to 188°C/370°F. Sprinkle the remaining sugar on top of the proofed pastries [8]. Bake the pastries for about 25 to 30 minutes until they are golden brown [9]. Remove the ring molds [10, 11]. Let the pastries cool slightly before serving.

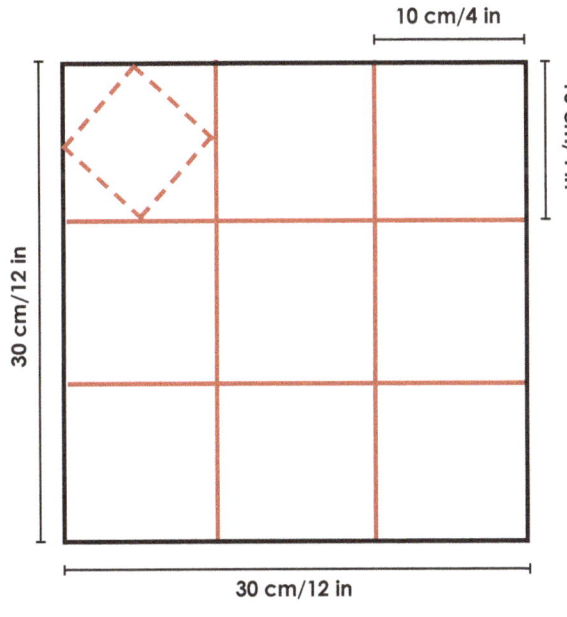

CLASSIC CHARMS

KOUIGN-AMANN

PAINS SUISSES

PAINS SUISSES

Another popular item on the menu of a French boulangerie is pain suisse, also known as the Swiss brioche. Eggs and butter add to the richness of this brioche, which is shaped like a rectangle and stuffed with vanilla cream and chocolate. This version of this specialty is made from crunchy croissant dough and is even more marvelous than the original offering.

Yield: 8 individual pastries

INGREDIENTS

760 g/1.7 lb croissant dough (page 8)

Vanilla Pastry Cream:

30 g/1.1 oz egg yolks

25 g/0.88 oz granulated sugar (A)

12 g/0.42 oz cornstarch

150 g/5.3 oz whole milk

25 g/0.88 oz granulated sugar (B)

1 vanilla bean

20 g/0.71 oz unsalted butter

Baking Finishes:

90 g/3.2 oz dark chocolate chips

1 egg

10 g/0.35 oz (2 tsp) heavy cream

Follow the recipe on page 8 to make a croissant dough. Take one of three portions of the dough (weighs about 760 g/1.7 lb) and cover it with plastic wrap. Reserve the dough in the refrigerator until you are ready to use it.

Vanilla Pastry Cream:

Combine the egg yolks, sugar (A), and cornstarch in a mixing bowl. Mix well with a balloon whisk. Set aside.

Place the milk and sugar (B) in a medium-sized saucepan. Use a paring knife to split the vanilla bean lengthwise. Scrape off the vanilla seeds using the back of the knife. Add the vanilla bean halves and seeds to the saucepan.

Heat the milk mixture over medium-high heat. Remove it from the heat when it comes to a boil. Pour the hot liquid into the reserved egg yolk mixture while whisking vigorously.

Pour the mixture back into the pan. Cook the mixture over medium-low heat while whisking constantly for 1 to 2 minutes until the mixture thickens. Remove the vanilla bean halves. Stir in the butter and mix well.

Cover the surface of the vanilla pastry cream with plastic wrap. Store it in the refrigerator if you are not using it immediately. Use it at room temperature.

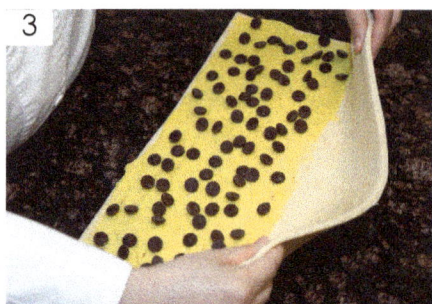

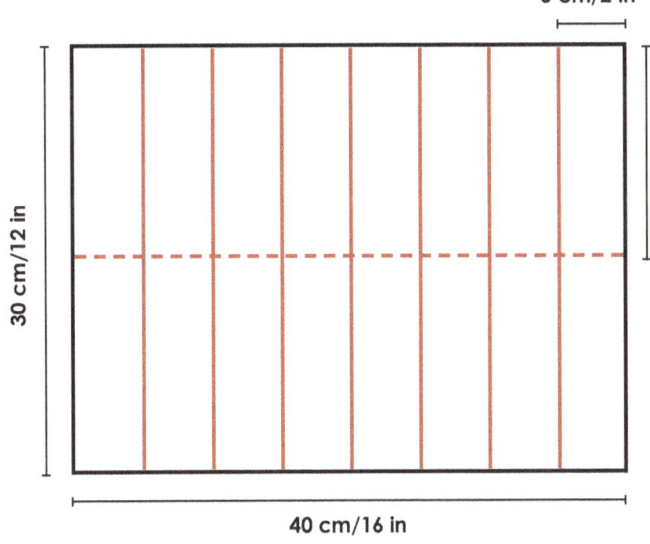

Shaping and Baking:

Roll out the croissant dough into a rectangle that is slightly larger than 40-cm x 30-cm/16-in x 12-in in size. Trim off the uneven edges.

Facing the longer edge, spread the vanilla pastry cream on the bottom half of the dough [1]. Scatter the dark chocolate chips on top [2]. Fold down the top half to form a 40-cm x 15-cm/16-in x 6-in rectangle [3, 4].

Cut the dough into eight strips, each 5-cm x 15-cm/2-in x 6-in [5].

Place the shaped pastries on a baking pan lined with parchment paper while leaving ample space among the pieces [6]. Cover with plastic wrap, and allow the pieces to proof for 1.5 to 2.5 hours or until doubled in volume at room temperature.

Meanwhile, preheat the oven to 188°C/370°F. In a bowl, whisk the egg with the heavy cream. Brush the pastries gently with the egg wash [7]. Take care not to cover the layers with egg wash.

Bake the pastries for about 20 to 25 minutes until they are golden brown [8, 9]. Let them cool slightly before serving.

CLASSIC CHARMS

PISTACHIO-RAISIN SNAILS

A pastry snail is also known as a pain aux raisins. It is made by rolling up a sheet of croissant dough around a velvety pastry cream and plump raisins and then cutting the dough packet into individual sections and baking them. Snails are my mother's favorite pastries. Whenever we have a chance to visit Paris, we make a pilgrimage to *Du Pain et Des Idées* to sample the boulangerie's famous pistachio-chocolate snails. The smell of freshly baked snails brings back beautiful memories of the time we spent together. This version of the snail, filled with pistachio pastry cream and raisins, is a pistachio lover's dream come true.

Yield: 9 individual pastries

INGREDIENTS

760 g/1.7 lb croissant dough (page 8)

Pistachio Pastry Cream:

30 g/1.1 oz egg yolks

20 g/0.71 oz granulated sugar (A)

12 g/0.42 oz cornstarch

130 g/4.6 oz whole milk

20 g/0.71 oz granulated sugar (B)

40 g/1.4 oz pistachio paste

15 g/0.53 oz unsalted butter

Baking Finishes:

80 g/2.8 oz raisins

1 egg

10 g/0.35 oz (2 tsp) heavy cream

Follow the recipe on page 8 to make a croissant dough. Take one of three portions of the dough (weighs about 760 g/1.7 lb) and cover it with plastic wrap. Reserve the dough in the refrigerator until you are ready to use it.

Pistachio Pastry Cream:

Combine the egg yolks, sugar (A), and cornstarch in a mixing bowl. Mix well with a balloon whisk. Set aside.

Place the milk and sugar (B) in a medium-sized saucepan. Heat the milk mixture over medium-high heat. Remove it from the heat when it comes to a boil. Pour the hot liquid into the reserved egg yolk mixture while whisking vigorously [1].

Pour the mixture back into the pan [2]. Cook the mixture over medium-low heat while whisking constantly for 1 to 2 minutes until the mixture thickens [3]. Stir in the pistachio paste and butter, and mix well [4].

Cover the surface of the pistachio pastry cream with plastic wrap. Store it in the refrigerator if you are not using it immediately. Use it at room temperature.

Shaping and Baking:

Roll out the croissant dough into a rectangle that is slightly larger than 23-cm x 40-cm/9-in x 16-in in size. Trim off the uneven edges.

Facing the shorter edge, spread the pistachio pastry cream on top of the dough, leaving a space of about 2.5-cm/1-in on top [5].

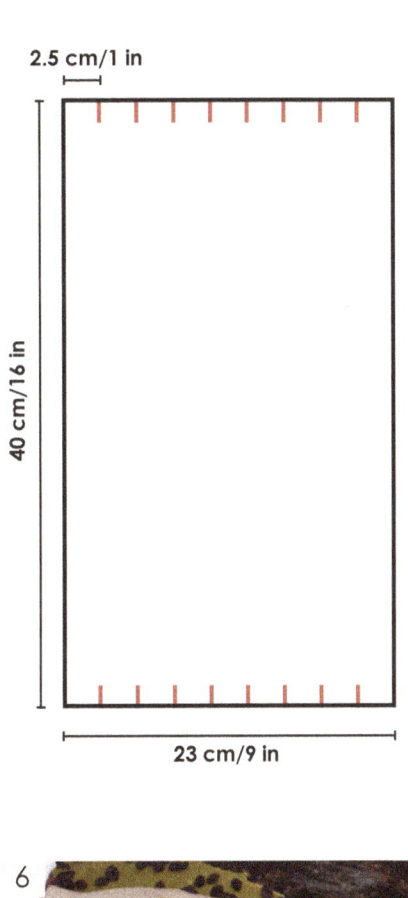

Scatter the raisins on top of the pastry cream. Brush the top edge with water [6]. Roll up the dough into a log [7, 8], and make sure the top edge adheres to the roll itself.

Freeze the log for about 15 minutes. Use a chef's knife to slice the dough into discs that are 2.5-cm/1-in in thickness [9]. There will be a total of nine discs.

Place the shaped pastries on a baking pan lined with parchment paper while leaving ample space among the pieces. Cover with plastic wrap, and allow the pieces to proof for 1.5 to 2.5 hours or until doubled in volume at room temperature.

Meanwhile, preheat the oven to 188°C/370°F. In a bowl, whisk the egg with the heavy cream. Brush the pastries gently with the egg wash [10]. Take care not to cover the layers with egg wash. Bake the pastries for about 20 to 25 minutes until they are golden brown [11]. Let them cool slightly before serving.

SNAIL FEVER

PISTACHIO-RAISIN SNAILS

CARAMEL-WALNUT SNAILS

CARAMEL-WALNUT SNAILS

Freshly baked warm snails filled with caramel pastry cream and crunchy walnuts are incredibly irresistible! This is an interesting variation of the snail that could be your favorite.

Yield: 9 individual pastries

INGREDIENTS

760 g/1.7 lb croissant dough (page 8)

Caramel Pastry Cream:

30 g/1.1 oz egg yolks

5 g/0.18 oz (2 tsp) cornstarch

80 g/2.8 oz whole milk

80 g/2.8 oz heavy cream

Pinch of salt

50 g/1.8 oz granulated sugar

15 g/0.53 oz unsalted butter

Baking Finishes:

80 g/1.8 oz walnut pieces

1 egg

10 g/0.35 oz (2 tsp) heavy cream

Follow the recipe on page 8 to make a croissant dough. Take one of three portions of the dough (weighs about 760 g/1.7 lb) and cover it with plastic wrap. Reserve the dough in the refrigerator until you are ready to use it.

Caramel Pastry Cream:

Combine the egg yolks and the cornstarch in a mixing bowl. Mix well with a balloon whisk [1]. Set aside.

To make the caramel, place the milk, heavy cream, and salt in a medium-sized saucepan. Heat the milk mixture over high heat. Remove the pan from the heat when the mixture comes to a boil. Reserve.

Place the sugar in a large saucepan in an even layer. Dry melt the sugar over medium heat undisturbed for 2 to 4 minutes. When most of the sugar underneath the top layer of granules is melted and has turned a golden color, reduce the heat to low. Stir occasionally with a spatula to avoid burning the caramel. When all of the sugar is melted and the caramel turns a medium-dark amber color [2], pour the reserved hot milk-cream mixture into the pan [3]. Stir vigorously to smooth out any lumps.

Pour the hot caramel liquid into the reserved egg yolk mixture while whisking vigorously [4]. Pour the mixture back into the pan [5]. Cook the mixture over medium-low heat while whisking constantly for 1 to 2 minutes until the mixture thickens [6]. Stir in the butter and mix well. Cover the surface of the caramel pastry cream with plastic wrap. Store it in the refrigerator if you are not using it immediately. Use it at room temperature.

Shaping and Baking:

Roll out the croissant dough into a rectangle that is slightly larger than 23-cm x 40-cm/9-in x 16-in in size. Trim off the uneven edges. Facing the shorter edge, spread the caramel pastry cream on top of the dough [7], leaving a space of about 2.5-cm/1-in on top.

Scatter the walnut pieces on top of the pastry cream. Brush the top edge with water. Roll up the dough into a log [8] and make sure the top edge adheres to the roll itself.

Freeze the log for about 15 minutes. Use a chef's knife to slice the dough into discs that are 2.5-cm/1-in in thickness [9]. There will be a total of nine discs.

Place the shaped pastries on a baking pan lined with parchment paper while leaving ample space among the pieces. Cover with plastic wrap, and allow the pieces to proof for 1.5 to 2.5 hours or until doubled in volume at room temperature.

Meanwhile, preheat the oven to 188°C/370°F. In a bowl, whisk the egg with the heavy cream. Brush the pastries gently with the egg wash [10]. Take care not to cover the layers with egg wash. Bake the pastries for about 20 to 25 minutes until they are golden brown [11]. Let them cool slightly before serving.

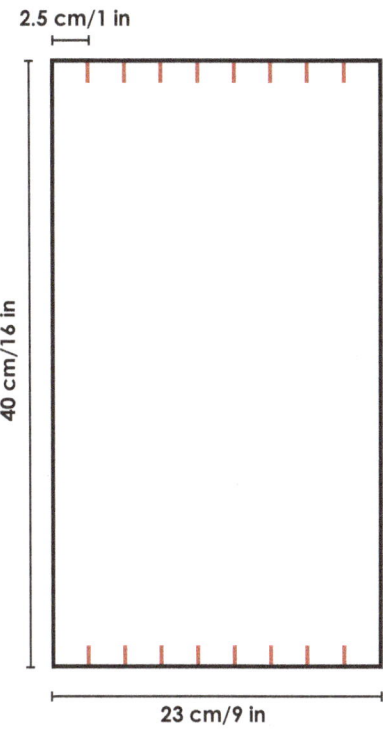

SNAIL FEVER   **55**

VANILLA SNAIL MUFFINS

These muffins are shaped to showcase their beautiful layers. Inside each muffin, you will find luscious, smooth vanilla buttercream. They are truly a symphony of beauty and taste.

Yield: 6 individual pastries

INGREDIENTS

760 g/1.7 lb croissant dough (page 8)

Vanilla Buttercream:

100 g/3.5 oz unsalted butter, at room temperature

100 g/3.5 oz cream cheese, at room temperature

40 g/1.4 oz granulated sugar

5 g/0.18 oz (1 tsp) vanilla extract

Baking Finishes:

Granulated sugar

Follow the recipe on page 8 to make a croissant dough. Take one of three portions of the dough (weighs about 760 g/1.7 lb) and cover it with plastic wrap. Reserve the dough in the refrigerator until you are ready to use it.

Vanilla Buttercream:

Combine the butter, cream cheese, sugar, and vanilla extract in a mixer bowl. Attach the bowl to a stand mixer fitted with a whisk attachment. Whisk until the cream is light and smooth. Cover the bowl with plastic wrap. Store the cream in the refrigerator if you are not using it immediately. Use it at room temperature.

Shaping and Baking:

Roll out the croissant dough into a rectangle that is slightly larger than 54-cm x 20-cm/21-in x 8-in in size. Trim off the uneven edges.

Cut the dough into three pieces, each 18-cm x 20-cm/7-in x 8-in [1].

Take a piece of the dough and brush the dough with water [2]. Facing the longer edge, roll up the dough into a log of 20-cm/8-in in length [3], and make sure the top edge adheres to the roll itself. Repeat to finish rolling the remaining two pieces of the dough [4].

Freeze the logs for about 15 minutes. Use a chef's knife to slice each log lengthwise in half [5]. There will be a total of six half-logs.

Place a half-log with the cut-side down on the table, roll up the dough [6, 7]. Repeat to finish shaping the remaining dough pieces.

Butter a large muffin pan (6-muffin capacity). Place the shaped pastries in the muffin pan [8]. Cover with plastic wrap, and allow the pieces to proof for 1.5 to 2.5 hours or until doubled in volume at room temperature.

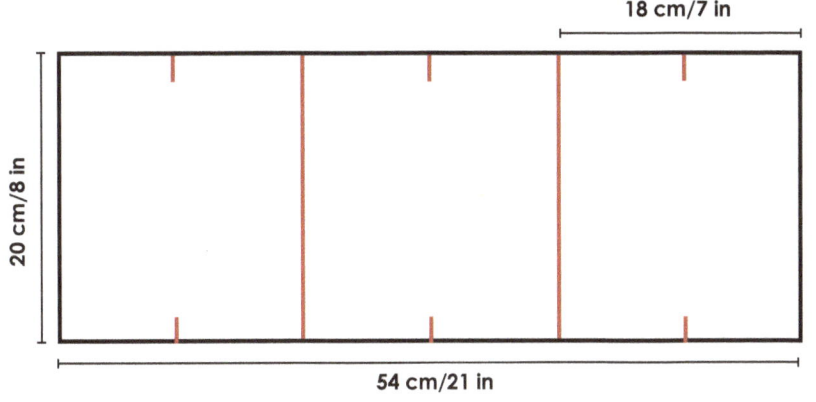

Meanwhile, preheat the oven to 188°C/370°F.

Bake the muffins for about 25 to 30 minutes until they are golden brown [9]. Remove the muffins from the baking pan. Roll the muffins in granulated sugar [10]. Let them cool completely before continuing.

Assembly:

Fill a large pastry bag fitted with a fine star tip (#864) of 1-cm/0.38-in with the vanilla buttercream. Pipe the filling into the muffins through the bottom [11].

SNAIL FEVER

VANILLA SNAIL MUFFINS

SESAME SNAIL PAIRS

SESAME SNAIL PAIRS

The sesame snail pair is shaped by rolling up two ends of a sheet of croissant dough and then twisting it in the middle to form an "S" configuration. The filling is made by adding sesame paste to pastry cream. The familiar croissant aroma is elevated with a roasted sesame fragrance to make an even more tempting pastry!

Yield: 9 individual pastries

INGREDIENTS

760 g/1.7 lb croissant dough (page 8)

Sesame Pastry Cream:

30 g/1.1 oz egg yolks

25 g/0.88 oz granulated sugar (A)

12 g/0.42 oz cornstarch

130 g/4.6 oz whole milk

25 g/0.88 oz granulated sugar (B)

40 g/1.4 oz unsweetened sesame paste

15 g/0.53 oz unsalted butter

Baking Finishes:

1 egg

10 g/0.35 oz (2 tsp) heavy cream

Mixed sesame seeds

Follow the recipe on page 8 to make a croissant dough. Take one of three portions of the dough (weighs about 760 g/1.7 lb) and cover it with plastic wrap. Reserve the dough in the refrigerator until you are ready to use it.

Sesame Pastry Cream:

Combine the egg yolks, sugar (A), and cornstarch in a mixing bowl. Mix well with a balloon whisk. Set aside.

Place the milk and sugar (B) in a medium-sized saucepan. Heat the milk mixture over medium-high heat. Remove it from the heat when it comes to a boil. Pour the hot liquid into the reserved egg yolk mixture while whisking vigorously.

Pour the mixture back into the pan. Cook the mixture over medium-low heat while whisking constantly for 1 to 2 minutes until the mixture thickens. Stir in the sesame paste and butter, and mix well. Cover the surface of the sesame pastry cream with plastic wrap. Store it in the refrigerator if you are not using it immediately. Use it at room temperature.

Shaping and Baking:

Roll out the croissant dough into a rectangle that is slightly larger than 23-cm x 40-cm/9-in x 16-in in size. Trim off the uneven edges.

Facing the shorter edge, spread the sesame pastry cream on the top and bottom portions of the dough sheet, leaving a space of about 3-cm/1.2-in in the middle [1]. Roll up the bottom edge [2], and then roll down the top edge while leaving a space of about 2.5-cm/1-in in the middle [3, 4].

Freeze the shaped dough for about 15 minutes. Use a chef's knife to slice the dough into

double-discs that are 2.5-cm/1-in in thickness [5]. There will be a total of nine double-discs.

If the piece is still too cold to bend, wait a few minutes. Take one piece of the double-discs and twist the bottom disc to form an "S" shape [6, 7]. Repeat to finish shaping the remaining pastry pieces [8].

Place the shaped pastries on a baking pan lined with parchment paper while leaving ample space among the pieces. Cover with plastic wrap, and allow the pieces to proof for 1.5 to 2.5 hours or until doubled in volume at room temperature.

Meanwhile, preheat the oven to 188°C/370°F. In a bowl, whisk the egg with the heavy cream. Brush the pastries gently with the egg wash [9]. Take care not to cover the layers with egg wash. Sprinkle the top with mixed sesame seeds [10]. Bake the pastries for about 20 to 25 minutes until they are golden brown [11]. Let them cool slightly before serving.

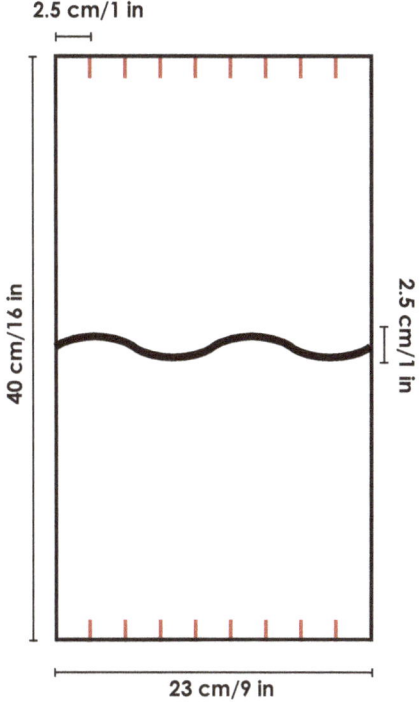

SNAIL FEVER

STRAWBERRY-CHOCOLATE SNAILS

This version of the snail is filled with strawberry pastry cream and chocolate chips. It is slightly on the sweeter side. The fruity strawberry fragrance complements the rich, dark chocolate splendidly, and together they are embraced by layers of buttery, crispy goodness.

Yield: 9 individual pastries

INGREDIENTS

760 g/1.7 lb croissant dough (page 8)

Strawberry Pastry Cream:

30 g/1.1 oz egg yolks

20 g/0.71 oz granulated sugar (A)

12 g/0.42 oz cornstarch

90 g/3.2 oz strawberry puree

30 g/1.1 oz whole milk

30 g/1.1 oz heavy cream

20 g/0.71 oz granulated sugar (B)

15 g/0.53 oz unsalted butter

Baking Finishes:

90 g/3.2 oz dark chocolate chips

1 egg

10 g/0.35 oz (2 tsp) heavy cream

Follow the recipe on page 8 to make a croissant dough. Take one of three portions of the dough (weighs about 760 g/1.7 lb) and cover it with plastic wrap. Reserve the dough in the refrigerator until you are ready to use it.

Strawberry Pastry Cream:

Combine the egg yolks, sugar (A), and cornstarch in a mixing bowl. Mix well with a balloon whisk [1]. Set aside.

Place the strawberry puree, milk, cream, and sugar (B) in a medium-sized saucepan. Heat the puree mixture over medium-high heat. Remove it from the heat when it comes to a boil. Pour the hot liquid into the reserved egg yolk mixture while whisking vigorously [2].

Pour the mixture back into the pan [3]. Cook the mixture over medium-low heat while whisking constantly for 1 to 2 minutes until the mixture thickens [4]. Stir in the butter and mix well.

Cover the surface of the strawberry pastry cream with plastic wrap. Store it in the refrigerator if you are not using it immediately. Use it at room temperature.

Shaping and Baking:

Roll out the croissant dough into a rectangle that is slightly larger than 23-cm x 40-cm/9-in x 16-in in size. Trim off the uneven edges.

Facing the shorter edge, spread the strawberry pastry cream on top of the dough, leaving a space of about 2.5-cm/1-in on top [5].

Scatter the chocolate chips on top of the pastry cream. Roll up the dough into a log [6]. Brush the top edge with water [7] and make sure the top edge adheres to the roll itself.

Freeze the log for about 15 minutes. Use a chef's knife to slice the dough into discs that are 2.5-cm/1-in in thickness [8]. There will be a total of nine discs.

Place the shaped pastries on a baking pan lined with parchment paper while leaving ample space among the pieces [9]. Cover with plastic wrap, and allow the pieces to proof for 1.5 to 2.5 hours or until doubled in volume at room temperature.

Meanwhile, preheat the oven to 188°C/370°F.

In a bowl, whisk the egg with the heavy cream. Brush the pastries gently with the egg wash [10]. Take care not to cover the layers with egg wash.

Bake the pastries for about 20 to 25 minutes until they are golden brown [11]. Let them cool slightly before serving.

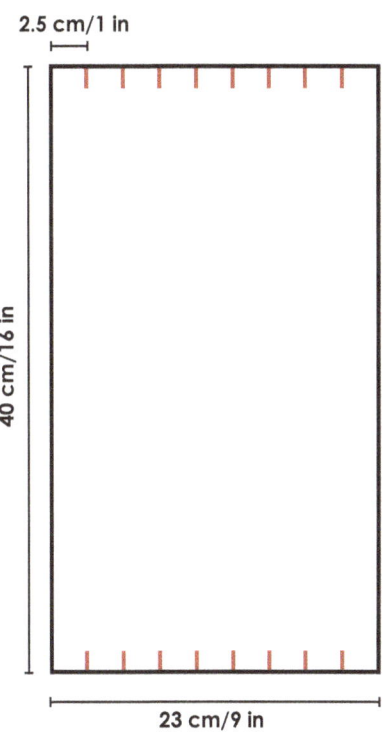

SNAIL FEVER

STRAWBERRY-CHOCOLATE SNAILS

SFOGLIATELLE

SFOGLIATELLE

The sfogliatella is a famous pastry specialty from the city of Naples and its surrounding region. This delectable version of the sfogliatella is made with flaky croissant dough stuffed with the traditional ricotta-orange filling.

Yield: 12 individual pastries

INGREDIENTS

760 g/1.7 lb croissant dough (page 8)

Ricotta Cheese Filling:

200 g/7.1 oz whole milk

60 g/2.1 oz granulated sugar

80 g/2.8 oz semolina flour

230 g/8.1 oz ricotta cheese

60 g/2.1 oz candied orange peels, chopped

1 egg (about 50 g/1.8 oz)

0.5 g/0.018 oz (¼ tsp) cinnamon powder

5 g/0.18 oz (1 tsp) vanilla extract

Baking Finishes:

Powdered sugar for dusting

Follow the recipe on page 8 to make a croissant dough. Take one of three portions of the dough (weighs about 760 g/1.7 lb) and cover it with plastic wrap. Reserve the dough in the refrigerator until you are ready to use it.

Ricotta Cheese Filling:

Place the milk and sugar in a medium-sized saucepan. Bring the mixture to a boil. Stir in the semolina flour [1]. Whisk the mixture constantly for 1 to 2 minutes until the mixture thickens [2]. Transfer the mixture to a mixer bowl. Let it cool completely before continuing.

Add the ricotta cheese, candied orange peels, egg, cinnamon powder, and vanilla extract into the mixer bowl. Attach the bowl to a stand mixer fitted with a paddle attachment. Mix all the ingredients until they are well combined [3].

Cover the filling with plastic wrap. Reserve the filling in the refrigerator until you are ready to use it.

Shaping and Baking:

Roll out the croissant dough into a rectangle that is slightly larger than 24-cm x 40-cm/9.5-in x 16-in in size. Trim off the uneven edges.

Brush the dough with water [4]. Facing the shorter edge, roll up the dough into a log [5], and make sure the top edge adheres to the roll itself.

Freeze the log for about 15 minutes. Use a chef's knife to slice the dough into discs that are 2-cm/0.8-in in thickness [6]. There will be a total of twelve discs.

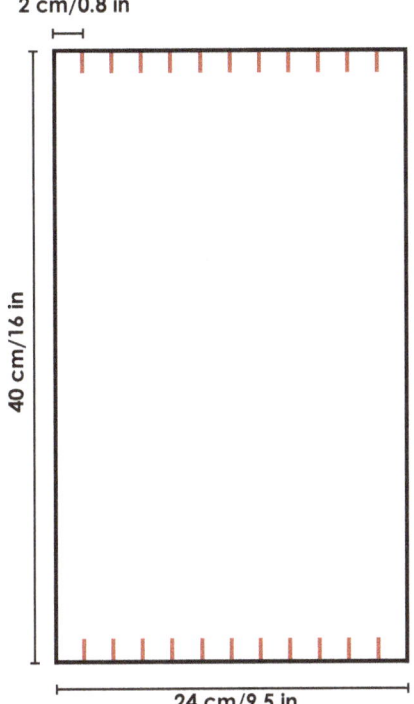

Take a disc and gently stretch it into a cone [7]. Place a spoon full of the ricotta cheese filling inside the cone [8]. Fold the cone so that the pastry resembles a shell [9]. Repeat to finish shaping the remaining dough pieces.

Place the shaped pastries on a baking pan lined with parchment paper while leaving ample space among the pieces [10]. Cover with plastic wrap, and allow the pieces to proof for 1.5 to 2.5 hours or until doubled in volume at room temperature.

Meanwhile, preheat the oven to 188°C/370°F.

Bake the pastries for about 20 minutes until they are golden brown. Dust the pastries with powdered sugar [11]. Let them cool slightly before serving.

SNAIL FEVER

VANILLA DOUBLE SNAILS

The vanilla double snail is formed by rolling up two ends of a sheet of croissant dough to form two rolls that meet in the middle. It resembles a pair of eyeglasses. The simple yet elegant vanilla-flavored pastry cream produces a classic that never goes out of style.

Yield: 9 individual pastries

INGREDIENTS

760 g/1.7 lb croissant dough (page 8)

Vanilla Pastry Cream:

30 g/1.1 oz egg yolks

25 g/0.88 oz granulated sugar (A)

12 g/0.42 oz cornstarch

150 g/5.3 oz whole milk

25 g/0.88 oz granulated sugar (B)

1 vanilla bean

20 g/0.71 oz unsalted butter

Baking Finishes:

1 egg

10 g/0.35 oz (2 tsp) heavy cream

Follow the recipe on page 8 to make a croissant dough. Take one of three portions of the dough (weighs about 760 g/1.7 lb) and cover it with plastic wrap. Reserve the dough in the refrigerator until you are ready to use it.

Vanilla Pastry Cream:

Combine the egg yolks, sugar (A), and cornstarch in a mixing bowl. Mix well with a balloon whisk [1]. Set aside.

Place the milk and sugar (B) in a medium-sized saucepan. Use a paring knife to split the vanilla bean lengthwise. Scrape off the vanilla seeds using the back of the knife. Add the vanilla bean halves and seeds to the saucepan.

Heat the milk mixture over medium-high heat. Remove it from the heat when it comes to a boil. Pour the hot liquid into the reserved egg yolk mixture while whisking vigorously [2].

Pour the mixture back into the pan [3]. Cook the mixture over medium-low heat while whisking constantly for 1 to 2 minutes until the mixture thickens [4]. Remove the vanilla bean halves. Stir in the butter and mix well.

Cover the surface of the vanilla pastry cream with plastic wrap. Store it in the refrigerator if you are not using it immediately. Use it at room temperature.

Shaping and Baking:

Roll out the croissant dough into a rectangle that is slightly larger than 23-cm x 40-cm/9-in x 16-in in size. Trim off the uneven edges.

Facing the shorter edge, spread the vanilla pastry cream over the entire dough sheet [5].

Roll up the bottom edge halfway [6], and then roll down the top edge so that the two rolls meet in the middle [7].

Freeze the shaped dough for about 15 minutes. Use a chef's knife to slice the dough into double-discs that are 2.5-cm/1-in in thickness [8]. There will be a total of nine double-discs.

Place the shaped pastries on a baking pan lined with parchment paper while leaving ample space among the pieces [9]. Cover with plastic wrap, and allow the pieces to proof for 1.5 to 2.5 hours or until doubled in volume at room temperature.

Meanwhile, preheat the oven to 188°C/370°F. In a bowl, whisk the egg with the heavy cream. Brush the pastries gently with the egg wash [10]. Take care not to cover the layers with egg wash. Bake the pastries for about 20 to 25 minutes until they are golden brown [11]. Let them cool slightly before serving.

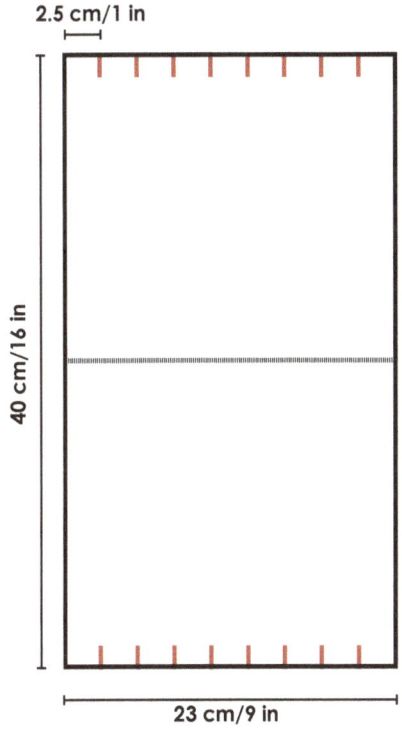

SNAIL FEVER

VANILLA DOUBLE SNAILS

PIZZA SNAILS

PIZZA SNAILS

The pizza snail is perfect for those who prefer savory over sweet. This unique creation is filled with tangy, herby tomato sauce and aged parmesan cheese. It is wonderful and can be enjoyed with any meal.

Yield: 9 individual pastries

INGREDIENTS

760 g/1.7 lb croissant dough (page 8)

Pizza Filling:

80 g/2.8 oz tomato sauce

50 g/1.8 oz grated parmesan cheese

Baking Finishes:

1 egg

10 g/0.35 oz (2 tsp) heavy cream

Follow the recipe on page 8 to make a croissant dough. Take one of three portions of the dough (weighs about 760 g/1.7 lb).

Roll out the croissant dough into a rectangle that is slightly larger than 23-cm x 40-cm/9-in x 16-in in size [1]. Trim off the uneven edges.

Facing the shorter edge, spread the tomato sauce on top of the dough [2], leaving a space of about 2.5-cm/1-in on top.

Sprinkle the grated parmesan cheese on top of the tomato sauce [3]. Roll up the dough into a log [4-6]. Brush the top edge with water [7] and make sure the top edge adheres to the roll itself.

Freeze the log for about 15 minutes. Use a chef's knife to slice the dough into discs that are 2.5-cm/1-in in thickness [8]. There will be a total of nine discs.

Place the shaped pastries on a baking pan lined with parchment paper while leaving ample space among the pieces [9]. Cover with plastic wrap, and allow the pieces to proof for 1.5 to 2.5 hours or until doubled in volume at room temperature.

Meanwhile, preheat the oven to 188°C/370°F.

In a bowl, whisk the egg with the heavy cream. Brush the pastries gently with the egg wash [10]. Take care not to cover the layers with egg wash.

Bake the pastries for about 20 to 25 minutes until they are golden brown [11, 12]. Let them cool slightly before serving.

SNAIL FEVER 73

FIG CIRCLES

A fig circle is an elegant yet simple croissant creation topped with homemade fig jam and crunchy almonds. Indeed, it is another delightful croissant dough offering that is pleasing to the eye and the taste buds.

Yield: 9 individual pastries

INGREDIENTS

760 g/1.7 lb croissant dough (page 8)

Fig Jam:

70 g/2.5 oz granulated sugar

2 g/0.071 oz (½ tsp) powdered pectin

170 g/6 oz fig puree

Baking Finishes:

1 egg

10 g/0.35 oz (2 tsp) heavy cream

Almond slices

Follow the recipe on page 8 to make a croissant dough. Take one of three portions of the dough (weighs about 760 g/1.7 lb) and cover it with plastic wrap. Reserve the dough in the refrigerator until you are ready to use it.

Fig Jam:

Combine half of the sugar (35 g/1.2 oz) and the pectin in a mixing bowl. Mix them thoroughly and reserve.

In a medium-sized saucepan, combine the fig puree with the remaining sugar (35 g/1.2 oz). Bring the mixture to a boil over medium-high heat. Stir in the sugar-pectin mixture [1]. Bring the mixture back to a boil and reduce the heat to medium-low. Stir constantly and cook for another 5 minutes [2].

Let the mixture cool slightly. Cover the surface of the jam with plastic wrap and store the jam in the refrigerator until you are ready to use it.

Shaping and Baking:

Roll out the croissant dough to about 30-cm x 30-cm/12-in x 12-in in size. Use a 10-cm/4-in round cutter to cut out nine pieces of the dough [3].

Place the shaped pastries on a baking pan lined with parchment paper while leaving ample space among the pieces. Cover with plastic wrap, and allow the pieces to proof for 1.5 to 2.5 hours or until doubled in volume at room temperature [4].

Meanwhile, preheat the oven to 188°C/370°F.

Use the back of a round spoon to press the center of each piece [5].

In a bowl, whisk the egg with the heavy cream. Brush the pastries gently with the egg wash [6]. Take care not to cover the layers with egg wash.

Place the fig jam in a medium-sized piping bag. Pipe a small amount of jam onto the center of each piece of dough [7]. Sprinkle almond slices on top [8]. Repeat to finish filling the remaining dough pieces.

Bake the pastries for about 20 to 25 minutes until they are golden brown [9, 10]. Let them cool slightly before serving.

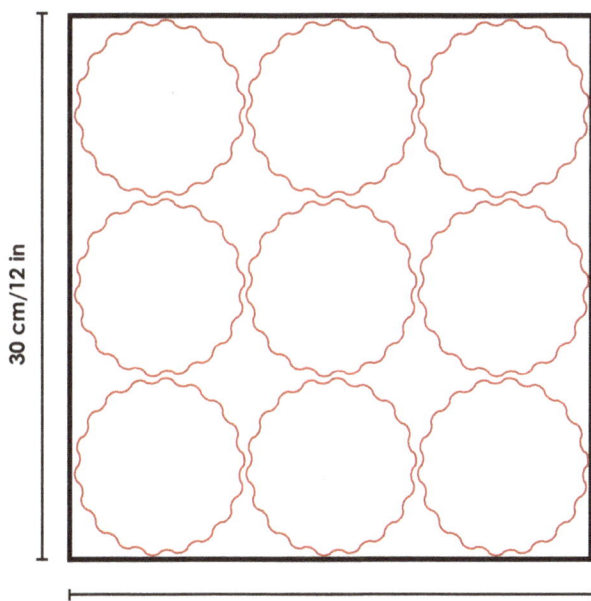

DANISH RETRO

FIG CIRCLES

CINNAMON SWIRLS

CINNAMON SWIRLS

Inspired by Swedish cinnamon buns, these warm, crunchy swirls of croissant pastry are bursting with the aromas of cinnamon and cardamom. The caramelized sugar makes them even more scrumptious.

Yield: 9 individual pastries

INGREDIENTS

760 g/1.7 lb croissant dough (page 8)

Cinnamon-Sugar Filling:

80 g/2.8 oz granulated sugar

4 g/0.14 oz (2 tsp) cinnamon powder

2 g/0.071 oz (1 tsp) cardamom powder

Baking Finishes:

1 egg

10 g/0.35 oz (2 tsp) heavy cream

Pearl sugar

Follow the recipe on page 8 to make a croissant dough. Take one of three portions of the dough (weighs about 760 g/1.7 lb) and cover it with plastic wrap. Reserve the dough in the refrigerator until you are ready to use it.

Cinnamon-Sugar Filling:

In a mixing bowl, combine the sugar, cinnamon powder, and cardamom powder. Mix well and reserve.

Shaping and Baking:

Roll out the croissant dough into a rectangle that is slightly larger than 23-cm x 50-cm/9-in x 20-in in size. Trim off the uneven edges.

Facing the shorter edge, brush the dough with water [1]. Sprinkle the cinnamon-sugar mixture on top of the dough [2]. Fold down the top half of the dough to form a 23-cm x 25-cm/9-in x 10-in rectangle [3].

Cut the dough into nine strips, each 2.5-cm x 25-cm/1-in x 10-in [4]. Take a dough strip, twist both ends [5], coil it into a disc [6], and tug the end underneath the disc itself [7]. Repeat to shape the remaining pieces [8].

Place the shaped pastries on a baking pan lined with parchment paper while leaving ample space among the pieces. Cover with plastic wrap, and allow the pieces to proof for 1.5 to 2.5 hours or until doubled in volume at room temperature.

Meanwhile, preheat the oven to 188°C/370°F.

In a bowl, whisk the egg with the heavy cream. Brush the pastries gently with the egg wash [9]. Take care not to cover the layers with egg wash.

Sprinkle the pearl sugar on top [10]. Bake the pastries for about 20 to 25 minutes until they are golden brown [11]. Let them cool slightly before serving.

DANISH RETRO 81

BLUEBERRY PINWHEELS

A traditionally shaped danish has been reinvented using croissant dough. Crispy layers are topped with rich, smooth cream cheese and fruity blueberry jam in the center, and the pastry is then whimsically transformed into a pinwheel.

Yield: 9 individual pastries

INGREDIENTS

760 g/1.7 lb croissant dough (page 8)

Blueberry Jam:

80 g/2.8 oz granulated sugar

2 g/0.071 oz (½ tsp) powdered pectin

170 g/6 oz blueberry puree

Cream Cheese Filling:

150 g/5.3 oz cream cheese, at room temperature

30 g/1.1 oz granulated sugar

10 g/0.35 oz (2 tsp) vanilla extract

Zest of one lemon

Baking Finishes:

1 egg

10 g/0.35 oz (2 tsp) heavy cream

Follow the recipe on page 8 to make a croissant dough. Take one of three portions of the dough (weighs about 760 g/1.7 lb) and cover it with plastic wrap. Reserve the dough in the refrigerator until you are ready to use it.

Blueberry Jam:

Combine half of the sugar (40 g/1.4 oz) and the pectin in a mixing bowl. Mix thoroughly and reserve.

In a medium-sized saucepan, combine the blueberry puree with the remaining sugar (40 g/1.4 oz). Bring the mixture to a boil over medium-high heat. Stir in the sugar-pectin mixture. Bring the mixture back to a boil and reduce the heat to medium-low. Stir constantly and cook for another 5 minutes.

Let the mixture cool slightly. Cover the surface of the jam with plastic wrap and store the jam in the refrigerator until you are ready to use it.

Cream Cheese Filling:

Combine the cream cheese, sugar, vanilla extract, and lemon zest in a mixing bowl. Mix well with a spoon. Cover the bowl with plastic wrap. Store the filling in the refrigerator until you are ready to use it.

Shaping and Baking:

Roll out the croissant dough into a square that is slightly larger than 30-cm x 30-cm/12-in x 12-in in size. Trim off the uneven edges. Cut the dough into nine squares, each 10-cm x 10-cm/4-in x 4-in [1].

Take a piece of the dough and use the tip of the knife to mark a dot in the center as a reference [2]. Position the tip of the knife 1.3-cm/0.5-in away from the center. Make a cut between that point and one of the corners. Make three more cuts on the remaining corners [3]. Brush the center with water. Lift the right tip of one of the triangular segments and fold it toward the center [4]. Repeat with the remaining three triangular segments [5].

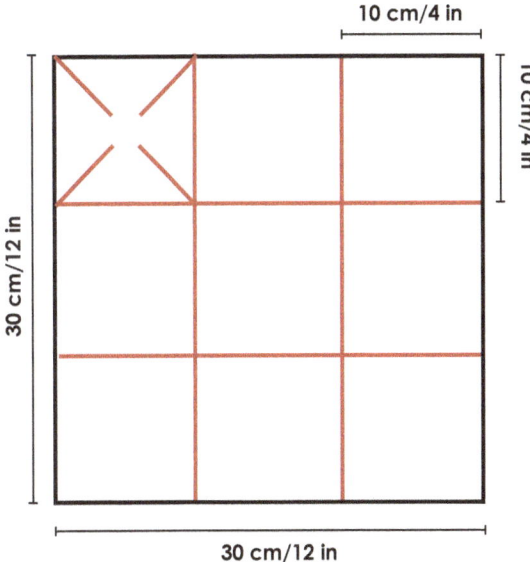

Place the shaped pastries on a baking pan lined with parchment paper while leaving ample space among the pieces. Cover with plastic wrap, and allow the pieces to proof for 1.5 to 2.5 hours or until doubled in volume at room temperature.

Meanwhile, preheat the oven to 188°C/370°F.

In a bowl, whisk the egg with the heavy cream. Brush the pastries gently with the egg wash. Take care not to cover the layers with egg wash.

Use the back of a round spoon to press the center of each piece [6]. Fill a medium-sized pastry bag with the cream cheese filling. Pipe a small amount of the filling onto the center [7]. Repeat to add the cream cheese filling to the remaining dough pieces.

Add the blueberry jam to the pastry bag, and pipe a small amount of jam on top of the cream cheese filling [8]. Repeat to finish filling the remaining dough pieces.

Bake the pastries for about 20 to 25 minutes until they are golden brown [9]. Let them cool slightly before serving.

DANISH RETRO

MUSHROOM TURNOVERS

MUSHROOM TURNOVERS

This traditional puff pastry delight is reinvented as a croissant creation. Its flaky and buttery exterior and its moist and tender interior conceal a savory and aromatic curry and mushroom surprise in its center.

Yield: 9 individual pastries

INGREDIENTS

760 g/1.7 lb croissant dough (page 8)

Mushroom-Curry Filling:

45 g/1.6 oz vegetable oil

10 g/0.35 oz curry powder

280 g/10 oz diced onions (about 2 small onions)

170 g/6 oz sliced baby portabella mushroom

2.5 g/0.088 oz (½ tsp) kosher salt

3 g/0.11 oz (1 tsp) cornstarch

15 g/0.53 oz water

Baking Finishes:

1 egg

10 g/0.35 oz (2 tsp) heavy cream

Follow the recipe on page 8 to make a croissant dough. Take one of three portions of the dough (weighs about 760 g/1.7 lb) and cover it with plastic wrap. Reserve the dough in the refrigerator until you are ready to use it.

Mushroom-Curry Filling:

Heat the oil in a sauté pan to 204°C/400°F over high heat. Add the curry powder to the pan. Stir constantly and fry the curry powder for a few seconds [1].

Add the diced onions and mushrooms [2]. Reduce to medium-low heat. Add the salt. Stir constantly and cook the mixture for about 10 minutes or until the onions and mushrooms are softened [3].

In a small bowl, mix the cornstarch with water. Add the mixture to the pan and stir. Cook for a few more seconds. Transfer the mushroom-curry filling to a bowl. Cover the bowl with plastic wrap. Reserve the filling in the refrigerator until you are ready to use it.

Shaping and Baking:

Roll out the croissant dough into a square that is slightly larger than 33-cm x 33-cm/13-in x 13-in in size. Trim off the uneven edges. Cut the dough into nine squares, each 11-cm x 11-cm/4.3-in x 4.3-in [4].

To make a design on the dough, freeze the dough pieces for 5 to 10 minutes. Position one piece of the dough in a diamond shape. Use a paring knife to score half of the dough piece [5]. Repeat to finish making the design for the remaining pieces.

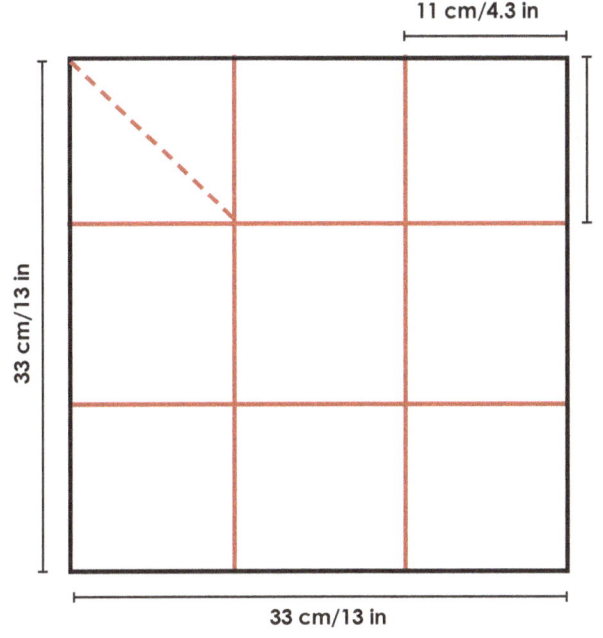

Turn over a piece of the dough, making sure the design will show on top after the piece is folded. If the dough is still too hard to be shaped, wait a few minutes.

Place a spoon full of the mushroom-curry filling on top of the dough. Brush the edge with water [6]. Fold the piece in half to enclose the filling to form a triangle. Press the edge to seal the turnover [7]. Repeat to finish forming the remaining dough pieces.

Place the shaped pastries on a baking pan lined with parchment paper while leaving ample space among the pieces. Cover with plastic wrap, and allow the pieces to proof for 1.5 to 2.5 hours or until doubled in volume at room temperature.

Meanwhile, preheat the oven to 188°C/370°F.

In a bowl, whisk the egg with the heavy cream. Brush the pastries gently with the egg wash [8]. Take care not to cover the layers with egg wash.

Bake the pastries for about 25 minutes until they are golden brown [9]. Let them cool slightly before serving.

APRICOT DIAMONDS

This delightful rendition of the traditional apricot danish is made of diamond-shaped croissant dough pieces topped with sweet, tangy apricots and crunchy sugar crystals. It's a familiar yet refreshing version of the classic.

Yield: 9 individual pastries

Ingredients

760 g/1.7 lb croissant dough (page 8)

1 egg

10 g/0.35 oz (2 tsp) heavy cream

9 apricot halves

Turbinado sugar (raw sugar crystals)

Follow the recipe on page 8 to make a croissant dough. Take one of three portions of the dough (weighs about 760 g/1.7 lb).

Roll out the croissant dough into a rectangle that is slightly larger than 32-cm x 24-cm/13-in x 9.4-in in size. Trim off the uneven edges.

Cut the dough horizontally into three strips, each the size of 32-cm x 8-cm/13-in x 3.1-in [1].

Take a dough strip and facing the long edge, use a knife to mark the dough at intervals of 9-cm/3.5-in on the bottom edge. Turn the dough 180 degrees, and repeat the marking of the dough at intervals of 9-cm/3.5-in on the bottom edge [2]. According to the guiding marks, make four diagonal cuts to create three diamond-shaped pieces [3-6]. Repeat to cut the remaining two strips of the dough [7].

Place the shaped pastries on a baking pan lined with parchment paper while leaving

ample space among the pieces. Cover with plastic wrap, and allow the pieces to proof for 1.5 to 2.5 hours or until doubled in volume at room temperature.

Meanwhile, preheat the oven to 188°C/370°F.

In a bowl, whisk the egg with the heavy cream. Brush the pastries gently with the egg wash [8]. Take care not to cover the layers with egg wash. Place an apricot half on top of each dough piece [9]. Sprinkle the top with raw sugar crystals [10].

Bake the pastries for about 20 to 25 minutes until they are golden brown [11, 12]. Let them cool slightly before serving.

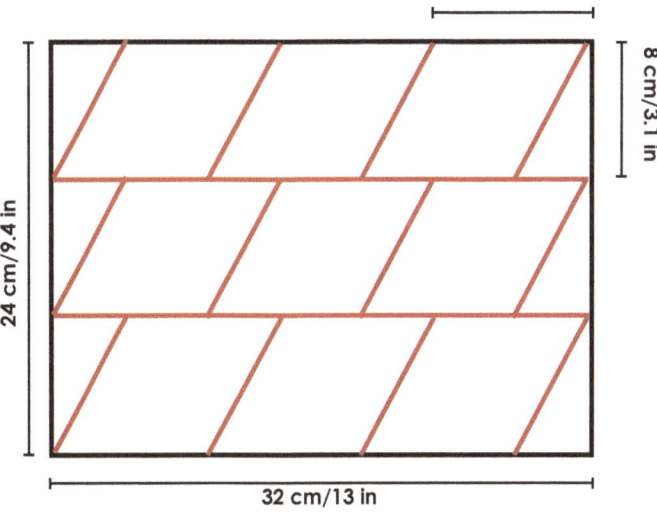

DANISH RETRO   89

APRICOT DIAMONDS

PISTACHIO-RASPBERRY TWISTS

PISTACHIO-RASPBERRY TWISTS

Delicious pistachio pastry cream topped with fresh raspberries, all stuffed in the middle of a whimsically shaped croissant pastry—another exquisite treat for any sweet tooth.

Yield: 10 individual pastries

INGREDIENTS

760 g/1.7 lb croissant dough (page 8)

Pistachio Pastry Cream:

30 g/1.1 oz egg yolks

20 g/0.71 oz granulated sugar (A)

12 g/0.42 oz cornstarch

130 g/4.6 oz whole milk

20 g/0.71 oz granulated sugar (B)

40 g/1.4 oz pistachio paste

15 g/0.53 oz unsalted butter

Baking Finishes:

1 egg

10 g/0.35 oz (2 tsp) heavy cream

Raspberries

Follow the recipe on page 8 to make a croissant dough. Take one of three portions of the dough (weighs about 760 g/1.7 lb) and cover it with plastic wrap. Reserve the dough in the refrigerator until you are ready to use it.

Pistachio Pastry Cream:

Combine the egg yolks, sugar (A), and cornstarch in a mixing bowl. Mix well with a balloon whisk. Set aside.

Place the milk and sugar (B) in a medium-sized saucepan. Heat the milk mixture over medium-high heat. Remove it from the heat when it comes to a boil. Pour the hot liquid into the reserved egg yolk mixture while whisking vigorously.

Pour the mixture back into the pan. Cook the mixture over medium-low heat while whisking constantly for 1 to 2 minutes until the mixture thickens. Stir in the pistachio paste and butter; mix well.

Cover the surface of the pistachio pastry cream with plastic wrap. Store in the refrigerator if you are not using it immediately. Use it at room temperature.

Shaping and Baking:

Roll out the croissant dough into a rectangle that is slightly larger than 25-cm x 32-cm/10-in x 13-in in size. Trim off the uneven edges.

Facing the shorter edge, cut the dough into ten pieces by making one horizontal cut and four vertical cuts [1]. Each piece is 5-cm x 16-cm/2-in x 6.3-in in size.

Take one piece of the dough and fold it in half into a rectangle of 5-cm x 8-cm/2-in x 3.1-in [2]. Make a vertical cut in the middle on the folded side that is about 6-cm/2.4-in in length [3].

To form the twist, first unfold the piece and then pick up the dough, fold one end over and through the opening [4-6], and finally fold the other end under and through the opening [7, 8].

Place the shaped pastries on a baking pan lined with parchment paper while leaving ample space among the pieces. Cover with plastic wrap, and allow the pieces to proof for 1.5 to 2.5 hours or until doubled in volume at room temperature.

Meanwhile, preheat the oven to 188°C/370°F. In a bowl, whisk the egg with the heavy cream. Brush the pastries gently with the egg wash. Take care not to cover the layers with egg wash.

Fill a medium-sized pastry bag with the pistachio pastry cream. Pipe a line of the pastry cream in the middle of each piece [9], and then place fresh raspberries on top of the filling [10]. Repeat to finish filling the remaining dough pieces. Bake the pastries for about 20 to 25 minutes until they are golden brown [11]. Let them cool slightly before serving.

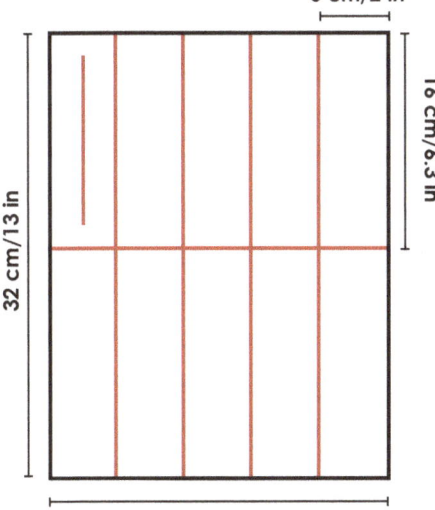

DANISH RETRO 93

PINEAPPLE SQUARES

An exotic pineapple-rum filling works wonders when paired with crunchy, buttery croissant layers. Pineapple squares are simple yet remarkable pastry treats that will please any discerning palate.

Yield: 9 individual pastries

INGREDIENTS

760 g/1.7 lb croissant dough (page 8)

Pineapple Compote:

50 g/1.8 oz unsalted butter

500 g/1.1 lb pineapple cubes

140 g/5 oz light brown sugar

15 g/0.53 oz dark rum

Baking Finishes:

1 egg

10 g/0.35 oz (2 tsp) heavy cream

Turbinado sugar (raw sugar crystals)

Follow the recipe on page 8 to make a croissant dough. Take one of three portions of the dough (weighs about 760 g/1.7 lb) and cover it with plastic wrap. Reserve the dough in the refrigerator until you are ready to use it.

Pineapple Compote:

Heat the butter in a saucepan over medium-high heat. Add the pineapple cubes [1] and sauté them for about 5 minutes.

Add the brown sugar [2] and continue to cook for another 5 minutes or until the pineapple cubes are softened and caramelized [3]. Deglaze the pan with the dark rum. Drain off excess liquid.

Transfer the pineapple compote into a bowl and let it cool. Cover the bowl with plastic wrap and store the compote in the refrigerator until you are ready to use it.

Shaping and Baking:

Roll out the croissant dough into a square that is slightly larger than 30-cm x 30-cm/12-in x 12-in in size. Trim off the uneven edges. Cut the dough into nine squares, each 10-cm x 10-cm/4-in x 4-in [4].

Place the shaped pastries on a baking pan lined with parchment paper while leaving ample space among the pieces. Cover with plastic wrap, and allow the pieces to proof for 1.5 to 2.5 hours or until doubled in volume at room temperature [5].

Meanwhile, preheat the oven to 188°C/370°F.

Use the back of a round spoon to press the center of each piece [6].

In a bowl, whisk the egg with the heavy cream. Brush the pastries gently with the egg wash [7]. Take care not to cover the layers with egg wash.

Place a spoonful of the pineapple compote in the center [8]. Sprinkle raw sugar crystals over the dough [9]. Repeat to finish filling the remaining dough pieces.

Bake the pastries for about 20 to 25 minutes until they are golden brown [10, 11]. Let them cool slightly before serving.

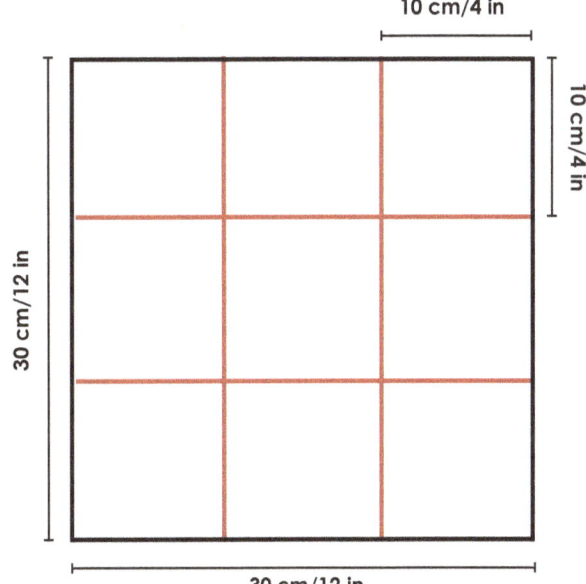

PINEAPPLE SQUARES

MAPLE-PECAN TWISTS

MAPLE-PECAN TWISTS

For this familiar danish classic, layers of twisted flaky croissant pastry are intertwined with luscious caramel pastry cream with a hint of maple essence and then topped with crunchy pecans.

Yield: 9 individual pastries

INGREDIENTS

760 g/1.7 lb croissant dough (page 8)

Maple-Caramel Pastry Cream:

30 g/1.1 oz egg yolks

5 g/0.18 oz (2 tsp) cornstarch

80 g/2.8 oz whole milk

80 g/2.8 oz heavy cream

Pinch of salt

50 g/1.8 oz granulated sugar

15 g/0.53 oz unsalted butter

5 g/0.18 oz (1 tsp) maple extract

Baking Finishes:

1 egg

10 g/0.35 oz (2 tsp) heavy cream

Pecan pieces

Follow the recipe on page 8 to make a croissant dough. Take one of three portions of the dough (weighs about 760 g/1.7 lb) and cover it with plastic wrap. Reserve the dough in the refrigerator until you are ready to use it.

Maple-Caramel Pastry Cream:

Combine the egg yolks and cornstarch in a mixing bowl. Mix well with a balloon whisk [1]. Set aside.

To make the caramel, place the milk, heavy cream, and salt in a medium-sized saucepan. Heat the milk mixture over high heat. Remove the pan from the heat when the mixture comes to a boil. Reserve.

Place the sugar in a large saucepan in an even layer. Dry melt the sugar over medium heat undisturbed for 2 to 4 minutes. When most of the sugar underneath the top layer of granules is melted and has turned a golden color, reduce the heat to low. Stir occasionally with a spatula to avoid burning the caramel.

When all of the sugar is melted and the caramel turns a medium-dark amber color [2], pour the reserved hot milk-cream mixture into the pan [3]. Stir vigorously to smooth out any lumps. Pour the hot caramel liquid into the reserved egg yolk mixture while whisking vigorously [4]. Pour the mixture back into the pan [5]. Cook the mixture over medium-low heat while whisking constantly for 1 to 2 minutes until the mixture thickens [6]. Stir in the butter and maple extract; mix well.

Cover the surface of the maple-caramel pastry cream with plastic wrap. Store it in the refrigerator if you are not using it immediately. Use it at room temperature.

Shaping and Baking:

Roll out the croissant dough into a rectangle that is slightly larger than 23-cm x 50-cm/9-in x 20-in in size. Trim off the uneven edges.

Facing the shorter edge, spread the maple-caramel pastry cream on the bottom half of the dough [7]. Fold down the top half of the dough to form a 23-cm x 25-cm/9-in x 10-in rectangle [8].

Cut the dough into nine 2.5-cm x 25-cm/1-in x 10-in strips [9]. Take a dough strip and twist both ends [10]. Repeat to shape the remaining pieces.

Place the shaped pastries on a baking pan lined with parchment paper while leaving ample space among the pieces. Cover with plastic wrap, and allow the pieces to proof for 1.5 to 2.5 hours or until doubled in volume at room temperature.

Meanwhile, preheat the oven to 188°C/370°F. In a bowl, whisk the egg with the heavy cream. Brush the pastries gently with the egg wash. Take care not to cover the layers with egg wash. Sprinkle pecan pieces on top [11]. Bake the pastries for about 20 to 25 minutes until they are golden brown. Let them cool slightly before serving.

TROPICAL DIAMONDS

A traditionally shaped danish pastry is made using the versatile croissant dough and topped with the intoxicating passionfruit and mango jam. It is an impressive creation that can be enjoyed at breakfast or as an after-meal dessert.

Yield: 9 individual pastries

INGREDIENTS

760 g/1.7 lb croissant dough (page 8)

Mango-Passion Jam:

80 g/2.8 oz granulated sugar

2 g/0.071 oz (½ tsp) pectin

100 g/3.5 oz mango puree

70 g/2.5 oz passionfruit puree

Baking Finishes:

1 egg

10 g/0.35 oz (2 tsp) heavy cream

Turbinado sugar (raw sugar crystals)

Follow the recipe on page 8 to make a croissant dough. Take one of three portions of the dough (weighs about 760 g/1.7 lb) and cover it with plastic wrap. Reserve the dough in the refrigerator until you are ready to use it.

Mango-Passion Jam:

Combine half of the sugar (40 g/1.4 oz) and the pectin in a mixing bowl. Mix thoroughly and reserve.

In a medium-sized saucepan, combine the mango and passionfruit purees with the remaining sugar (40 g/1.4 oz). Bring the mixture to a boil over medium-high heat. Stir in the sugar-pectin mixture. Bring the mixture back to a boil and reduce the heat to medium-low. Stir constantly and cook for another 5 minutes.

Let the mixture cool slightly. Cover the surface of the jam with plastic wrap and store the jam in the refrigerator until you are ready to use it.

Shaping and Baking:

Roll out the croissant dough into a square that is slightly larger than 30-cm x 30-cm/12-in x 12-in in size. Trim off the uneven edges. Cut the dough into nine squares, each 10-cm x 10-cm/4-in x 4-in [1].

Position a square as a diamond [2]. Lift the bottom corner and fold it up to align with the top corner and therefore form a triangle [3]. Position the tip of the knife 1.3-cm/0.5-in from the top corner of the triangle, and make a cut that is 1.3-cm/0.5-in away and parallel to the right edge [4]. Unfold the pastry dough [5]. Brush the left edge of the dough with water [6]. Pick up the right corner on the cut side and fold the cut border to the left [7] and stick it to the left edge [8]. Repeat to finish shaping the remaining pieces.

Place the shaped pastries on a baking pan lined with parchment paper while leaving ample space among the pieces. Cover with plastic wrap, and allow the pieces to proof for 1.5 to 2.5 hours or until doubled in volume at room temperature.

Meanwhile, preheat the oven to 188°C/370°F. In a bowl, whisk the egg with the heavy cream. Brush the pastries gently with the egg wash [9]. Take care not to cover the layers with egg wash.

Use the back of a round spoon to press the center of each piece. Add a spoonful of the mango-passionfruit jam in the center [10]. Repeat to finish filling the remaining dough pieces. Sprinkle the pastries with raw sugar crystals. Bake the pastries for about 20 to 25 minutes until they are golden brown [11]. Let them cool slightly before serving.

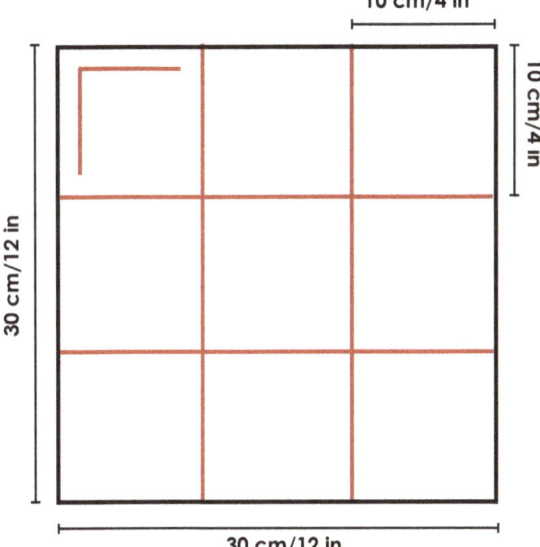

TROPICAL DIAMONDS

APRICOT POCKETS

APRICOT POCKETS

This danish classic is transformed into a morsel of deliciousness. Its lemon-accented cream cheese is topped with a sweet, tangy apricot jam, all wrapped around with warm, crackly layers of pastry dough.

Yield: 9 individual pastries

INGREDIENTS

760 g/1.7 lb croissant dough (page 8)

Apricot Jam:

80 g/2.8 oz granulated sugar

2 g/0.071 oz (½ tsp) powdered pectin

170 g/6 oz apricot puree

Cream Cheese Filling:

150 g/5.3 oz cream cheese, at room temperature

30 g/1.1 oz granulated sugar

10 g/0.35 oz (2 tsp) vanilla extract

Zest of one lemon

Baking Finishes:

1 egg

10 g/0.35 oz (2 tsp) heavy cream

Follow the recipe on page 8 to make a croissant dough. Take one of three portions of the dough (weighs about 760 g/1.7 lb) and cover it with plastic wrap. Reserve the dough in the refrigerator until you are ready to use it.

Apricot Jam:

Combine half of the sugar (40 g/1.4 oz) and the pectin in a mixing bowl. Mix thoroughly and reserve.

In a medium-sized saucepan, combine the apricot puree with the remaining sugar (40 g/1.4 oz). Bring the mixture to a boil over medium-high heat. Stir in the sugar-pectin mixture. Bring the mixture back to a boil and reduce the heat to medium-low. Stir constantly and cook for another 5 minutes.

Let the mixture cool slightly. Cover the surface of the jam with plastic wrap and store the jam in the refrigerator until you are ready to use it.

Cream Cheese Filling:

Combine the cream cheese, sugar, vanilla extract, and lemon zest in a mixing bowl. Mix well with a spoon. Cover the bowl with plastic wrap. Store the filling in the refrigerator until you are ready to use it.

Shaping and Baking:

Roll out the croissant dough into a square that is slightly larger than 30-cm x 30-cm/12-in x 12-in in size. Trim off the uneven edges. Cut the dough into nine squares, each 10-cm x 10-cm/4-in x 4-in [1].

Take a piece of the dough, and brush the center with water [2]. Fold one corner toward the center, and then fold the opposite corner on a diagonal toward the center [3]. Press on the dough so that the two tips adhere to the center [4].

Place the shaped pastries on a baking pan lined with parchment paper while leaving ample space among the pieces [5]. Cover with plastic wrap, and allow the pieces to proof for 1.5 to 2.5 hours or until doubled in volume at room temperature.

Meanwhile, preheat the oven to 188°C/370°F.

In a bowl, whisk the egg with the heavy cream. Brush the pastries gently with the egg wash. Take care not to cover the layers with egg wash.

Use the back of a round spoon to press the center of each piece [6]. Fill a medium-sized pastry bag with the cream cheese filling. Pipe a small amount of the filling onto the center [7]. Repeat to add the cream cheese filling to the remaining dough pieces.

Add the apricot jam to the pastry bag and pipe a small amount of jam on top of the cream cheese filling [8]. Repeat to finish filling the remaining dough pieces.

Bake the pastries for about 20 to 25 minutes until they are golden brown [9]. Let them cool slightly before serving.

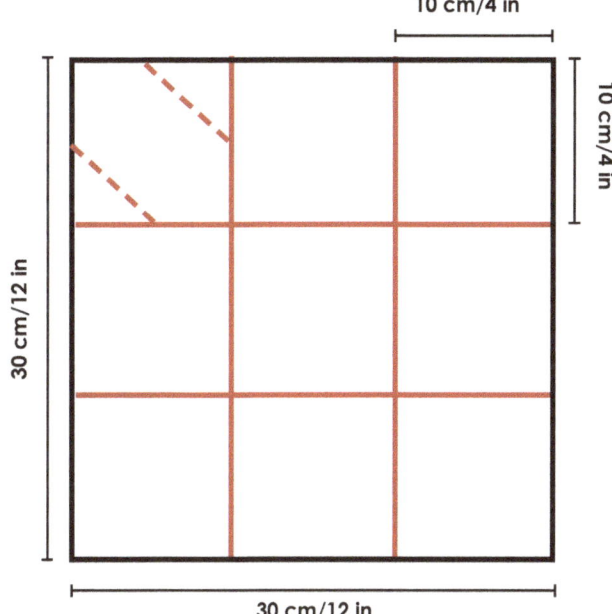

DANISH RETRO   105

MODERN CHIC

APPLE TREES

The classic flavors of autumn are transformed into this marvelous pastry. It has sweet caramel, tangy and fragrant apples, and a crunchy and buttery crumble, all surrounded by flaky, nutty layers of tree-shaped croissant dough. After just one bite, you will agree that it is a comforting yet stylish croissant creation.

Yield: 10 individual pastries

INGREDIENTS

760 g/1.7 lb croissant dough (page 8)

Caramel-Apple Compote:

40 g/1.4 oz heavy cream

80 g/2.8 oz granulated sugar

400 g/14 oz Granny Smith apple cubes

15 g/0.53 oz calvados (aged apple brandy)

Crumble Topping:

30 g/1.1 oz all-purpose flour

30 g/1.1 oz almond flour

30 g/1.1 oz granulated sugar

0.5 g/0.018 oz (¼ tsp) nutmeg powder

Pinch of salt

30 g/1.1 oz unsalted butter cubes, chilled

Baking Finishes:

1 egg

10 g/0.35 oz (2 tsp) heavy cream

Follow the recipe on page 8 to make a croissant dough. Take one of three portions of the dough (weighs about 760 g/1.7 lb) and cover it with plastic wrap. Reserve the dough in the refrigerator until you are ready to use it.

Apple Compote:

To make the caramel, place the heavy cream in a medium-sized saucepan. Heat the cream over high heat. Remove the pan from the heat when the cream comes to a boil. Reserve.

Place the sugar in a large saucepan in an even layer. Dry melt the sugar over medium heat undisturbed for 2 to 4 minutes [1]. When most of the sugar underneath the top layer of granules is melted and has turned a golden color, reduce the heat to low. Stir occasionally with a spatula to avoid burning the caramel.

When all of the sugar is melted and the caramel turns a medium-dark amber color, pour the hot cream into the pan [2]. Stir vigorously to smooth out any lumps.

Add the apple cubes to the pan [3]. Continue to cook the apples for another 8 to 10 minutes while stirring constantly [4]. Add the calvados to deglaze the pan. Stir to combine.

Transfer the caramel-apple compote to a bowl and let it cool. Cover the bowl with plastic wrap and store the compote in the refrigerator until you are ready to use it.

Crumble Topping:

Combine the flour, almond flour, sugar, nutmeg, and salt in a food processor bowl. Pulse the machine a few times to evenly distribute the ingredients. Add the chilled butter cubes. Pulse the machine a few more times until small pea-sized dough pieces are formed. Do not overmix.

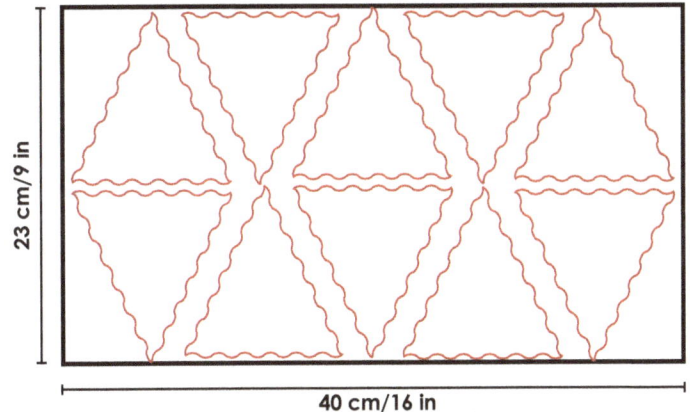

Line a baking sheet with parchment paper and spread the dough pieces on top of the parchment paper. Break up any remaining large pieces of dough. Cover the crumble with plastic wrap and store in the refrigerator until you are ready to use it.

Shaping and Baking:

Roll out the croissant dough to about 40-cm x 23-cm/16-in x 9-in in size. Use a tree-shaped cutter of 10-cm x 11-cm/4-in x 4.5-in in size to cut out ten pieces of the dough [5].

Place the shaped pastries on a baking pan lined with parchment paper while leaving ample space among the pieces. Cover with plastic wrap, and allow the pieces to proof for 1.5 to 2.5 hours or until doubled in volume at room temperature.

Meanwhile, preheat the oven to 188°C/370°F. In a bowl, whisk the egg with the heavy cream. Brush the pastries gently with the egg wash. Take care not to cover the layers with egg wash.

Use the back of a round spoon to press the center of each piece [6]. Place a spoonful of the apple compote in the center [7]. Sprinkle the crumble topping over the dough [8]. Repeat to finish filling the remaining dough pieces.

Bake the pastries for about 20 to 25 minutes until they are golden brown [9]. Let them cool slightly before serving.

MODERN CHIC

APPLE TREES

ROSE LOAVES

ROSE LOAVES

This beautifully woven braid reveals the effect of its laminated layers after it has been baked. It is then stuffed with a creamy, luscious rose-infused buttercream. It is truly a memorable modern croissant creation.

Yield: 5 individual pastries

Ingredients

760 g/1.7 lb croissant dough (page 8)

Rose Cream:

100 g/3.5 oz unsalted butter, at room temperature

100 g/3.5 oz cream cheese, at room temperature

40 g/1.4 oz granulated sugar

5 g/0.18 oz (1 tsp) rose extract

Baking Finishes:

1 egg

10 g/0.35 oz (2 tsp) heavy cream

Follow the recipe on page 8 to make a croissant dough. Take one of three portions of the dough (weighs about 760 g/1.7 lb) and cover it with plastic wrap. Reserve the dough in the refrigerator until you are ready to use it.

Rose Cream:

Add the softened butter, cream cheese, sugar, and rose extract in a mixer bowl.

Using a stand mixer fitted with a whisk attachment to whisk the mixture until it is light and fluffy [1]. Cover the bowl with plastic wrap. Store the cream in the refrigerator if you are not using it immediately. Use it at room temperature.

Shaping and Baking:

Roll out the croissant dough into a rectangle that is slightly larger than 30-cm x 20-cm/12-in x 8-in in size. Trim off the uneven edges.

Butter five mini loaf pans of 14-cm x 7.6-cm x 5-cm/5.5-in x 3-in x 2-in.

Cut the dough into five strips, each 6-cm x 20-cm/2.4-in x 8-in [2]. Take one piece of the dough, and while keeping an area of 1.3-cm/0.5-in intact on top, cut the strip into three strands [3]. Make a three-strand braid and pinch the ends together [4-6]. Place the braid into a buttered mini loaf pan. Repeat to finish forming the remaining dough pieces [7].

Place the loaf pans on a baking pan. Cover them with plastic wrap, and allow the pieces to proof for 1.5 to 2.5 hours or until doubled in volume at room temperature.

Meanwhile, preheat the oven to 188°C/370°F.

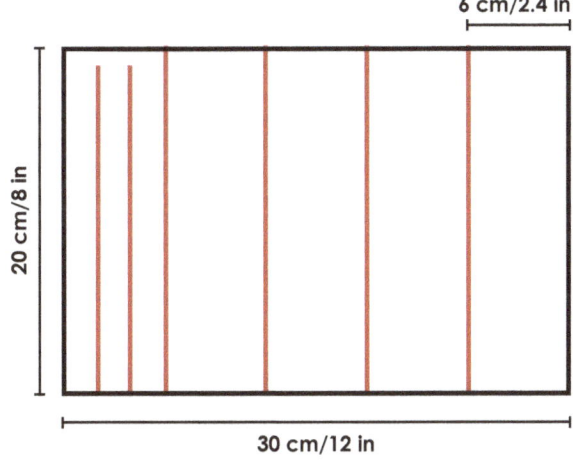

In a bowl, whisk the egg with the heavy cream. Brush the pastries gently with the egg wash [8]. Take care not to cover the layers with egg wash.

Bake the pastries for about 25 minutes until they are golden brown [9]. Unmold them from the loaf pans. Let them cool completely before continuing.

Assembly:

Fill a large pastry bag fitted with a fine star tip (#864) of 1-cm/0.38-in with the rose cream.

Use your thumb to press on the bottom of the loaf to make two or three holes. Pipe the filling into the loaf through the holes [10]. Repeat to finish filling the remaining loaves.

MEYER LEMON ROLLS

This stylish croissant pastry is stuffed with creamy, fragrant Meyer lemon cream and then glazed with tangy Meyer lemon icing. Accompanied by a pot of Earl Grey tea, this pastry makes a perfect afternoon refreshment.

Yield: 8 individual pastries

INGREDIENTS

760 g/1.7 lb croissant dough (page 8)

Meyer Lemon Cream:

2.5 g/0.088 oz gelatin sheet (one sheet of silver grade gelatin)

1 egg (about 50 g/1.8 oz)

60 g/2.1 oz granulated sugar

30 g/1.1 oz Meyer lemon juice

Zest of one Meyer lemon

70 g/2.5 oz unsalted butter, at room temperature

70 g/2.5 oz cream cheese, at room temperature

Baking Finishes:

120 g/4.2 oz powdered sugar

45 g/1.6 oz Meyer lemon juice

Follow the recipe on page 8 to make a croissant dough. Take one of three portions of the dough (weighs about 760 g/1.7 lb) and cover it with plastic wrap. Reserve the dough in the refrigerator until you are ready to use it.

Meyer Lemon Cream:

In a medium-sized bowl, bloom the sheet gelatin in plenty of cold water. Let the gelatin bloom for at least 5 minutes before using it.

Combine the egg, sugar, lemon juice, and lemon zest in a medium-sized saucepan. Heat the mixture over medium heat. Whisk the mixture constantly to allow even heating. Cook the mixture to 85°C/185°F and remove the pan from the heat [1]. Take care not to overheat the mixture; otherwise, the egg in the mixture will coagulate.

Meanwhile, squeeze the excess water out of the bloomed sheet gelatin and add the gelatin to the lemon mixture. Stir to combine.

Pass the mixture through a fine-mesh strainer. Cover the surface of the Meyer lemon mixture with plastic wrap. Let it cool completely.

Combine the Meyer lemon mixture, softened butter, and cream cheese in a mixer bowl. Attach the bowl to a stand mixer fitted with a whisk attachment. Whisk until the cream is light and smooth [2]. Cover the bowl with plastic wrap. Store the cream in the refrigerator if you are not using it immediately. Use it at room temperature.

Shaping and Baking:

Roll out the croissant dough into a rectangle that is slightly larger than 32-cm x 30-cm/13-in x 12-in in size. Trim off the uneven edges.

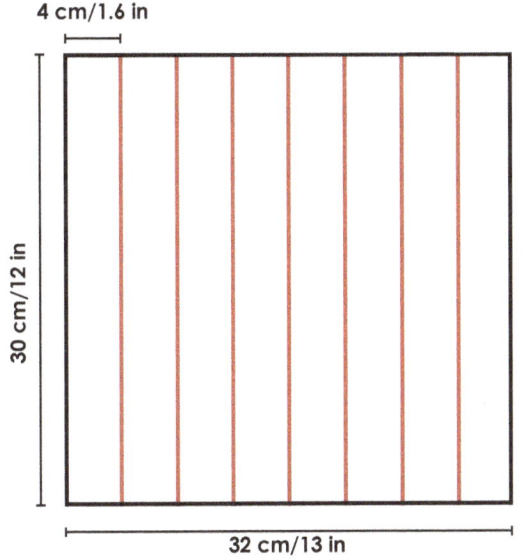

Cut the dough into eight strips, each 4-cm x 30-cm/1.6-in x 12-in [3]. Roll up each strip into a spiral [4]. Place the shaped pastries on a baking pan lined with parchment paper while leaving ample space among the pieces.

Butter eight ring molds, each 7.6-cm/3-in in diameter (5.7-cm/2.2-in in height). Place the ring molds around the dough pieces [5]. Cover with plastic wrap, and allow the pieces to proof for 1.5 to 2.5 hours or until doubled in volume at room temperature [6].

Meanwhile, preheat the oven to 188°C/370°F.

Bake the pastries for about 25 minutes until they are golden [7]. Remove the ring molds. Let them cool completely before continuing.

Assembly:

Fill a large pastry bag fitted with a fine star tip (#864) of 1-cm/0.38-in with the Meyer lemon filling. Use your thumb to press on the bottom of the roll to make a hole. Pipe the filling into the roll through the hole [8]. Repeat to finish filling the remaining rolls.

In a mixing bowl, combine the powdered sugar and Meyer lemon juice. Mix well. Dip the rolls in the lemon icing [9]. Allow the icing to set slightly before serving the pastries.

MEYER LEMON ROLLS

HAZELNUT SUNFLOWERS

HAZELNUT SUNFLOWERS

These beautiful sunflowers surely will satisfy the cravings of any pastry and art lover. Even van Gogh would be tempted by those flaky layers filled with a rich, nutty cream.

Yield: 6 individual pastries

INGREDIENTS

760 g/1.7 lb croissant dough (page 8)

Hazelnut Pastry Cream:

30 g/1.1 oz egg yolks

20 g/0.71 oz granulated sugar (A)

12 g/0.42 oz cornstarch

130 g/4.6 oz whole milk

20 g/0.71 oz granulated sugar (B)

40 g/1.4 oz hazelnut paste

15 g/0.53 oz unsalted butter

Baking Finishes:

1 egg

10 g/0.35 oz (2 tsp) heavy cream

Chocolate chips

Follow the recipe on page 8 to make a croissant dough. Take one of three portions of the dough (weighs about 760 g/1.7 lb) and cover it with plastic wrap. Reserve the dough in the refrigerator until you are ready to use it.

Hazelnut Pastry Cream:

Combine the egg yolks, sugar (A), and cornstarch in a mixing bowl. Mix well with a balloon whisk [1]. Set aside.

Place the milk and sugar (B) in a medium-sized saucepan. Heat the milk mixture over medium-high heat. Remove it from the heat when it comes to a boil. Pour the hot liquid into the reserved egg yolk mixture while whisking vigorously [2].

Pour the mixture back into the pan [3]. Cook the mixture over medium-low heat while whisking constantly for 1 to 2 minutes until the mixture thickens [4]. Stir in the hazelnut paste and butter; mix well [5].

Cover the surface of the hazelnut pastry cream with plastic wrap. Store the cream in the refrigerator if you are not using it immediately. Use it at room temperature.

Shaping and Baking:

Roll out the croissant dough to about 36-cm x 23-cm/14-in x 9-in in size. Use a snowflake-shaped cutter of 13-cm x 13-cm/5-in x 5-in in size to cut out six pieces of the dough [6, 7].

Place the shaped pastries on a baking pan lined with parchment paper while leaving ample space among the pieces. Cover with plastic wrap, and allow the pieces to proof for 1.5 to 2.5 hours or until doubled in volume at room temperature.

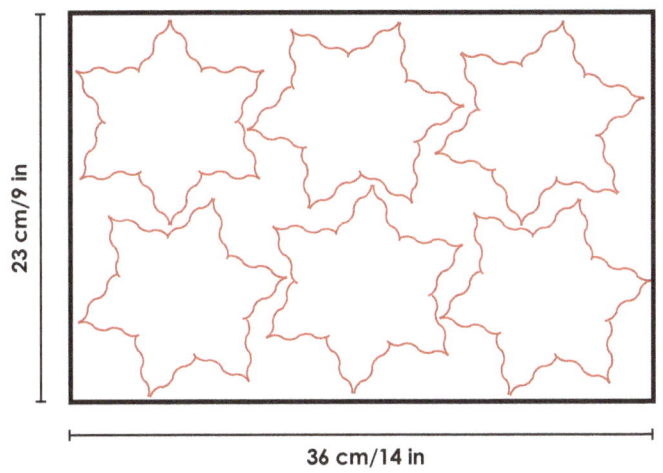

Meanwhile, preheat the oven to 188°C/370°F.

In a bowl, whisk the egg with the heavy cream. Brush the pastries gently with the egg wash. Take care not to cover the layers with egg wash.

Use the back of a round spoon to press the center of each piece [8]. Fill a medium-sized pastry bag with the hazelnut pastry cream. Pipe a small amount of the filling onto the center [9]. Place a few chocolate chips on top of the pastry cream. Repeat to finish filling the remaining dough pieces [10].

Bake the pastries for about 18 to 23 minutes until they are golden brown [11]. Let them cool slightly before serving.

CHERRY-ALMOND MUFFINS

This is not your ordinary muffin! These muffins are made from rich, buttery croissant dough and filled with almond cream that is bursting with fresh orange flavor. The pine nuts add an extra layer of complexity. It's all topped with a sweet cherry.

Yield: 9 individual pastries

INGREDIENTS

760 g/1.7 lb croissant dough (page 8)

Almond Cream:

140 g/4.9 oz cream cheese, at room temperature

140 g/4.9 oz almond paste

Zest of two oranges

15 g/0.53 oz (1 Tbsp) orange liqueur

50 g/1.8 oz pine nuts

Baking Finishes:

9 red cherries, pitted

Follow the recipe on page 8 to make a croissant dough. Take one of three portions of the dough (weighs about 760 g/1.7 lb) and cover it with plastic wrap. Reserve the dough in the refrigerator until you are ready to use it.

Almond Cream:

In a mixing bowl, combine the cream cheese, almond paste, orange zest, and orange liqueur. Mix all the ingredients into a paste using a spoon.

Add the pine nuts to the mixture. Mix well. Cover the bowl with plastic wrap. Store the filling in the refrigerator if you are not using it immediately. Use it at room temperature.

Shaping and Baking:

Roll out the croissant dough into a square that is slightly larger than 30-cm x 30-cm/12-in x 12-in in size. Trim off the uneven edges. Cut the dough into nine squares, each 10-cm x 10-cm/4-in x 4-in [1].

Butter nine ring molds [2], each 9-cm/3.5-in in diameter (5-cm/2-in in height). Place the molds on top of a baking pan lined with parchment paper [3].

Take a piece of the dough, and add a spoonful of the almond cream in the center [4]. Add a cherry on top [5]. Fold up the four corners of the dough piece. Place the shaped pastry inside a ring mold [6]. Repeat to finish shaping the remaining pieces [7].

Cover with plastic wrap, and allow the pieces to proof for 1.5 to 2.5 hours or until doubled in volume at room temperature.

Meanwhile, preheat the oven to 188°C/370°F.

Bake the pastries for about 20 to 25 minutes until they are golden brown. Remove them from the ring molds [8]. Let them cool slightly before serving.

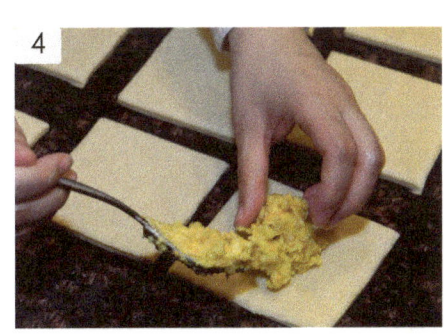

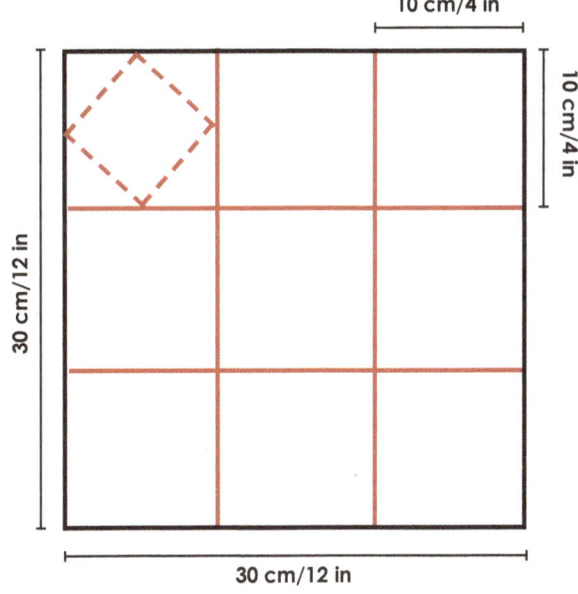

10 cm/4 in

10 cm/4 in

30 cm/12 in

30 cm/12 in

MODERN CHIC 121

CHERRY-ALMOND MUFFINS

ESPRESSO-CARAMEL LOAVES

ESPRESSO-CARAMEL LOAVES

These exquisite loaves are fashioned like an accordion to showcase their elegant layers. After baking, they are filled with velvety, smooth espresso-caramel cream. This beautiful modern croissant creation makes your next coffee break an extraordinary experience.

Yield: 5 individual pastries

INGREDIENTS

760 g/1.7 lb croissant dough (page 8)

Espresso-Caramel Cream:

60 g/2.1 oz espresso or strong coffee

70 g/2.5 oz granulated sugar

20 g/0.71 oz unsalted butter (A)

80 g/2.8 oz unsalted butter, at room temperature (B)

50 g/1.8 oz cream cheese, at room temperature

Baking Finishes:

Powdered sugar for dusting

Follow the recipe on page 8 to make a croissant dough. Take one of three portions of the dough (weighs about 760 g/1.7 lb) and cover it with plastic wrap. Reserve the dough in the refrigerator until you are ready to use it.

Espresso-Caramel Cream:

To make the caramel, place the espresso in a medium-sized saucepan. Heat the espresso over high heat. Remove the pan from the heat when the espresso comes to a boil. Reserve.

Place the sugar in a large saucepan in an even layer. Dry melt the sugar over medium heat undisturbed for 2 to 4 minutes. When most of the sugar underneath the top layer of granules is melted and has turned a golden color, reduce the heat to low. Stir occasionally with a spatula to avoid burning the caramel.

When all of the sugar is melted and the caramel turns a medium-dark amber color, pour the hot espresso into the pan [1, 2]. Stir vigorously to smooth out any lumps [3]. Add the butter (A). Transfer the espresso-caramel to a mixer bowl. Let it cool completely before continuing.

Add the softened butter (B) and cream cheese to the bowl. Using a stand mixer fitted with a whisk attachment to whisk the mixture until it is light and fluffy [4]. Cover the bowl with plastic wrap. Store the cream in the refrigerator if you are not using it immediately. Use it at room temperature.

Shaping and Baking:

Roll out the croissant dough into a rectangle that is slightly larger than 20-cm x 40-cm/8-in x 16-in in size. Trim off the uneven edges.

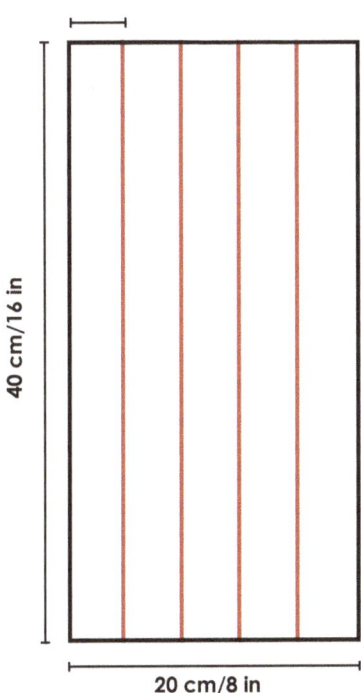

Butter five mini loaf pans, each 14-cm x 7.6-cm x 5-cm/5.5-in x 3-in x 2-in.

Cut the dough into five strips, each 4-cm x 40-cm/1.6-in x 16-in [5]. Take one strip, and fold the dough zig-zag style like an accordion [6]. Place the dough in a buttered mini loaf pan. Repeat to fold the remaining pieces [7].

Place the loaf pans on a baking pan. Cover with plastic wrap, and allow the pieces to proof for 1.5 to 2.5 hours or until doubled in volume at room temperature.

Meanwhile, preheat the oven to 188°C/370°F. Bake the pastries for about 25 minutes until they are golden brown. Unmold them from the loaf pans. Let them cool completely before continuing.

Assembly:

Fill a large pastry bag fitted with a fine star tip (#864) of 1-cm/0.38-in with the espresso-caramel cream.

Use your thumb to press on the bottom of the loaf to make two or three holes [8]. Pipe the filling into the loaf through the holes [9]. Repeat to finish filling the remaining loaves.

Dust the top of the loaves with powdered sugar [10].

APRICOT HEARTS

This Valentine's Day, entice your sweetheart with this decadent croissant creation. It's a warm, crispy heart-shaped croissant adorned with sweet, aromatic homemade apricot jam and buttery, spicy cookie crumbles. Who can resist such a sinfully delicious temptation?

Yield: 9 individual pastries

INGREDIENTS

760 g/1.7 lb croissant dough (page 8)

Apricot Jam:

80 g/2.8 oz granulated sugar

2 g/0.071 oz (½ tsp) powdered pectin

170 g/6 oz apricot puree

Crumble Topping:

30 g/1.1 oz all-purpose flour

30 g/1.1 oz almond flour

30 g/1.1 oz granulated sugar

0.5 g/0.018 oz (¼ tsp) nutmeg powder

Pinch of salt

30 g/1.1 oz unsalted butter cubes, chilled

Baking Finishes:

1 egg

10 g/0.35 oz (2 tsp) heavy cream

Follow the recipe on page 8 to make a croissant dough. Take one of three portions of the dough (weighs about 760 g/1.7 lb) and cover it with plastic wrap. Reserve the dough in the refrigerator until you are ready to use it.

Apricot Jam:

Combine half of the sugar (40 g/1.4 oz) and the pectin in a mixing bowl. Mix thoroughly and reserve.

In a medium-sized saucepan, combine the apricot puree with the remaining sugar (40 g/1.4 oz). Bring the mixture to a boil over medium-high heat. Stir in the sugar-pectin mixture [1]. Bring the mixture back to a boil and reduce the heat to medium-low. Stir constantly and cook for another 5 minutes [2].

Let the mixture cool slightly. Cover the surface of the jam with plastic wrap and store the jam in the refrigerator until you are ready to use it.

Crumble Topping:

Combine the flour, almond flour, sugar, nutmeg, and salt in a food processor bowl. Pulse the machine a few times to evenly distribute the ingredients.

Add the chilled butter cubes. Pulse the machine a few more times until small pea-sized dough pieces are formed [3]. Do not overmix.

Line a baking sheet with parchment paper, and spread the dough pieces on top of the parchment paper [4]. Break up any remaining large pieces of dough. Cover the crumble with plastic wrap and store it in the refrigerator until you are ready to use it.

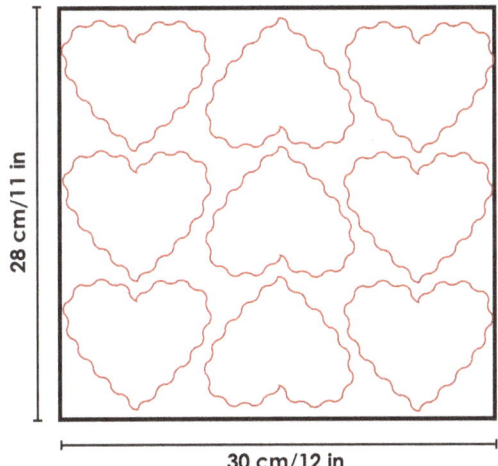

Shaping and Baking:

Roll out the croissant dough to about 30-cm x 28-cm/12-in x 11-in in size. Use a heart-shaped cutter of 10-cm x 9-cm/4-in x 3.5-in in size to cut out nine pieces of the dough [5].

Place the shaped pastries on a baking pan lined with parchment paper while leaving ample space among the pieces. Cover with plastic wrap, and allow the pieces to proof for 1.5 to 2.5 hours or until doubled in volume at room temperature.

Meanwhile, preheat the oven to 188°C/370°F.

In a bowl, whisk the egg with the heavy cream. Brush the pastries gently with the egg wash. Take care not to cover the layers with egg wash.

Use the back of a round spoon to press the center of each piece [6]. Fill a small pastry bag with the apricot jam. Pipe a small amount of the jam in the center [7]. Sprinkle the crumble topping over the dough [8]. Repeat to finish filling the remaining dough pieces.

Bake the pastries for about 20 to 25 minutes until they are golden brown [9]. Let them cool slightly before serving.

APRICOT HEARTS

MONT-BLANC

MONT-BLANC

Mont-blanc is a beloved French classic dessert featuring a sweet baked meringue covered with light Chantilly cream and chestnut paste in the form of vermicelli. This version of the mont-blanc is nothing short of a masterpiece. The beautifully rolled plump layers of croissant dough show off sophisticated cross sections in a peak. The pastry is filled with a rum-infused chestnut cream. What a remarkable and chic croissant creation!

Yield: 8 individual pastries

INGREDIENTS

760 g/1.7 lb croissant dough (page 8)

Chestnut Cream:

150 g/5.3 oz roasted chestnuts

40 g/1.4 oz granulated sugar

50 g/1.8 oz unsalted butter, at room temperature

50 g/1.8 oz cream cheese, at room temperature

25 g/0.88 oz dark rum

5 g/0.18 oz (1 tsp) vanilla extract

Baking Finishes:

Powdered sugar for dusting

Follow the recipe on page 8 to make a croissant dough. Take one of three portions of the dough (weighs about 760 g/1.7 lb) and cover it with plastic wrap. Reserve the dough in the refrigerator until you are ready to use it.

Chestnut Cream:

In a food processor bowl, combine the roasted chestnuts and sugar [1]. Pulse the machine a few times to break up the large pieces of chestnuts.

Add the softened butter, cream cheese, dark rum, and vanilla extract. Process the mixture into a paste [2].

Cover the surface of the chestnut cream with plastic wrap. Store the cream in the refrigerator if you are not using it immediately. Use it at room temperature.

Shaping and Baking:

Roll out the croissant dough into a rectangle that is slightly larger than 32-cm x 30-cm/13-in x 12-in in size. Trim off the uneven edges.

Cut the dough into eight strips, each 4-cm x 30-cm/1.6-in x 12-in [3]. Roll up each strip into a spiral [4, 5]. Place the shaped pastries on a baking pan lined with parchment paper while leaving ample space among the pieces [6].

Butter eight ring molds [7], each 7.6-cm/3-in in diameter (5.7-cm/2.2-in in height). Place the ring molds around the dough pieces [8]. Cover with plastic wrap, and allow the pieces to proof for 1.5 to 2.5 hours or until doubled in volume at room temperature.

Meanwhile, preheat the oven to 188°C/370°F. Bake the pastries for about 25 minutes until they are golden [9]. Remove the ring molds. Let them cool completely before continuing.

Assembly:

Fill a large pastry bag fitted with a fine star tip (#864) of 1-cm/0.38-in with the chestnut cream. Use your thumb to press on the bottom of the roll to make a hole [10]. Pipe the filling into the roll through the hole [11]. Repeat to finish filling the remaining rolls.

Dust the pastries with powdered sugar.

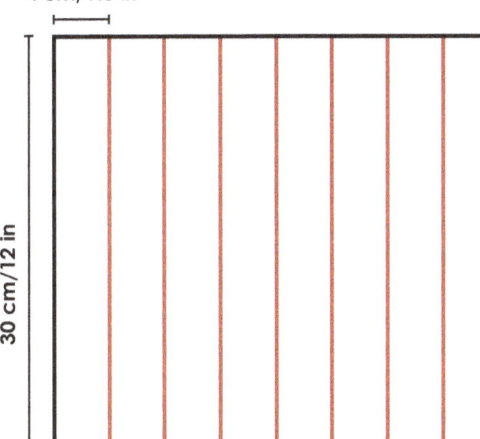

MODERN CHIC 131

CASSIS KNOTS

A cassis knot is a beautifully braided roll. Inside it you will find sweet, fruity homemade cassis jam. It's the perfect companion for your morning coffee or afternoon tea.

Yield: 8 individual pastries

INGREDIENTS

760 g/1.7 lb croissant dough (page 8)

Cassis Jam:

80 g/2.8 oz granulated sugar

2 g/0.071 oz (½ tsp) powdered pectin

170 g/6 oz cassis (black currant) puree

Baking Finishes:

1 egg

10 g/0.35 oz (2 tsp) heavy cream

Follow the recipe on page 8 to make a croissant dough. Take one of three portions of the dough (weighs about 760 g/1.7 lb) and cover it with plastic wrap. Reserve the dough in the refrigerator until you are ready to use it.

Cassis Jam:

Combine half of the sugar (40 g/1.4 oz) and the pectin in a mixing bowl. Mix thoroughly and reserve.

In a medium-sized saucepan, combine the cassis puree with the remaining sugar (40 g/1.4 oz). Bring the mixture to a boil over medium-high heat. Stir in the sugar-pectin mixture [1]. Bring the mixture back to a boil and reduce the heat to medium-low. Stir constantly and cook for another 5 minutes [2].

Let the mixture cool slightly. Cover the surface of the jam with plastic wrap and store the jam in the refrigerator until you are ready to use it.

Shaping and Baking:

Roll out the croissant dough into a rectangle that is slightly larger than 24-cm x 36-cm/9.4-in x 14-in in size. Trim off the uneven edges.

Use a knife to cut the dough into two strips, each 24-cm x 18-cm/9.4-in x 7-in in size. Cut each strip into four pieces, each 6-cm x 18-cm/2.4-in x 7-in in size. There will be a total of eight dough pieces.

Take one piece of the dough, and while keeping an area of 1.3-cm/0.5-in intact on top, cut the strip into three strands [3]. Make a three-strand braid and pinch the ends together [4, 5].

Fill a medium-sized pastry bag with the cassis jam. Pipe a row of the jam in the middle of each braided strand [6].

Roll up the dough onto itself with the jam enclosed in the center [7, 8]. Repeat to finish shaping the remaining pieces [9].

Place the shaped pastries on a baking pan lined with parchment paper while leaving ample space among the pieces. Cover with plastic wrap, and allow the pieces to proof for 1.5 to 2.5 hours or until doubled in volume at room temperature.

Meanwhile, preheat the oven to 188°C/370°F. In a bowl, whisk the egg with the heavy cream. Brush the pastries gently with the egg wash [10]. Take care not to cover the layers with egg wash.

Bake the pastries for about 20 to 25 minutes until they are golden brown [11]. Let them cool slightly before serving.

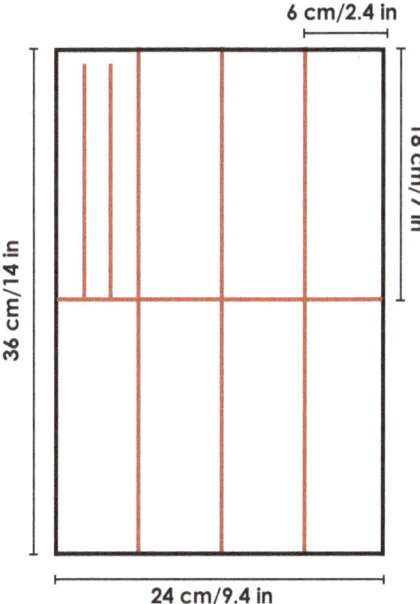

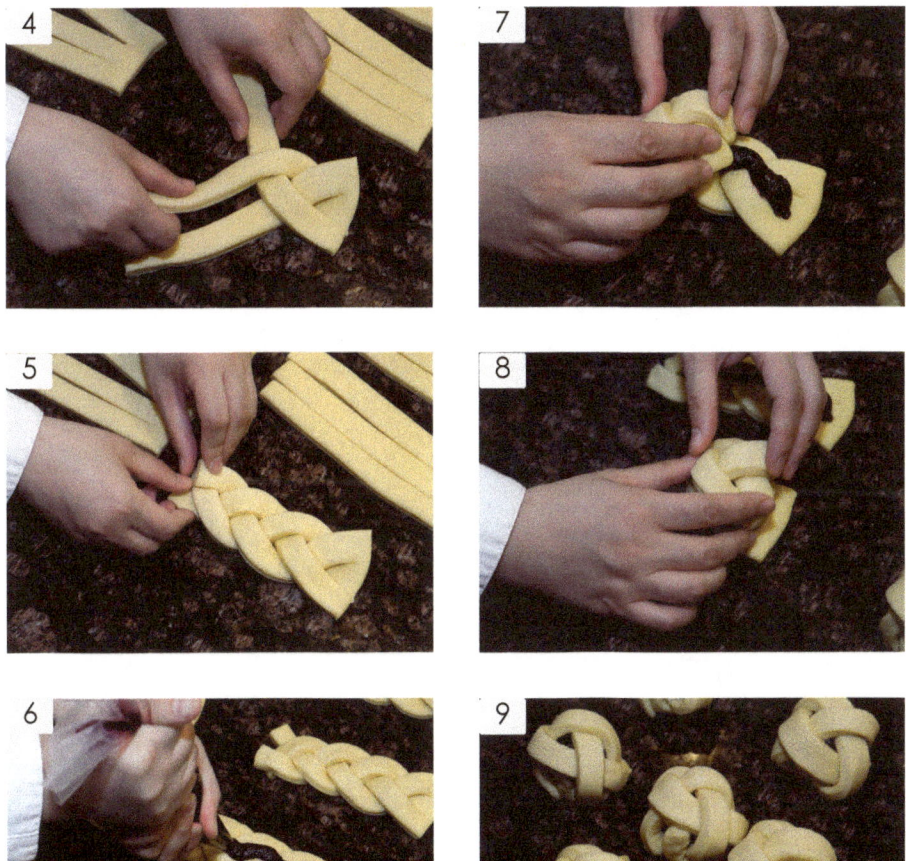

MODERN CHIC 133

WHISKEY TARTS

WHISKEY TARTS

A whiskey tart is a perfect dessert pastry. Its velvety, smooth filling packs a punch with the addition of bourbon whiskey, and it is surrounded by flaky layers of deliciousness.

Yield: 9 individual pastries

INGREDIENTS

760 g/1.7 lb croissant dough (page 8)

Whiskey Filling:

50 g/1.8 oz almond paste

50 g/1.8 oz sour cream

1 egg (about 50 g/1.8 oz)

25 g/0.88 oz granulated sugar

15 g/0.53 oz bourbon whiskey

Baking Finishes:

Powdered sugar for dusting

Follow the recipe on page 8 to make a croissant dough. Take one of three portions of the dough (weighs about 760 g/1.7 lb) and cover it with plastic wrap. Reserve the dough in the refrigerator until you are ready to use it.

Whiskey Filling:

In a mixing bowl, combine the almond paste, sour cream, egg, sugar, and bourbon whiskey. Blend the mixture using an immersion blender until it is homogenous [1, 2]. Cover the bowl with plastic wrap and reserve the mixture in the refrigerator until you are ready to use it.

Shaping and Baking:

Roll out the croissant dough to about 38-cm x 38-cm/15-in x 15-in in size. Using a 13-cm/5-in ring mold as a guide, cut out nine circles from the dough with a paring knife [3].

Butter nine tart rings, each 7.6-cm/3-in in diameter. Line the tart rings with the dough pieces [4].

Place the lined tart shells on a baking pan lined with parchment paper [5]. Cover with plastic wrap, and allow the pieces to proof for 1.5 to 2.5 hours or until doubled in volume at room temperature.

Meanwhile, preheat the oven to 188°C/370°F.

Use your finger to gently deflate the center of each proofed tart shell. Spoon the whiskey filling into the center of each to about ¾ full [6].

Bake the pastries for about 20 to 25 minutes until they are golden brown [7]. Remove the tart rings. Dust the top of each pastry with powdered sugar [8]. Let the pastries cool slightly before serving.

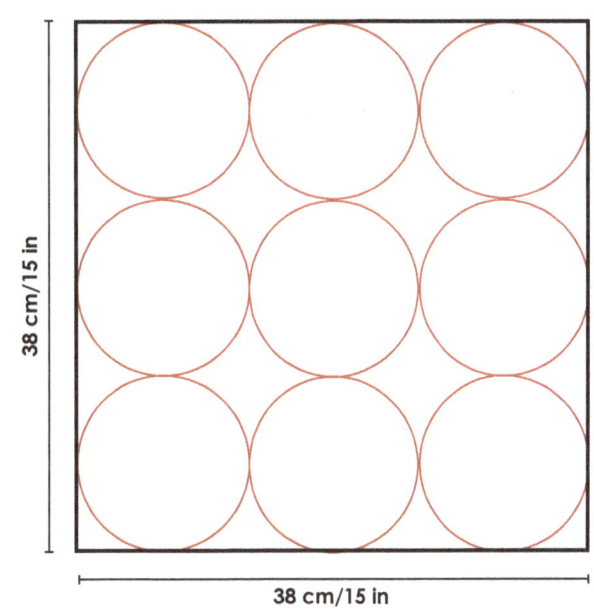

38 cm/15 in

38 cm/15 in

MODERN CHIC 137

BEAR CLAWS

This beloved danish classic is transformed into an extraordinary creation. The cardamom-lemon accented and kirsch-infused sweet almond filling oozes out of the crispy, luscious layers of the rich croissant dough. The turbinado sugar and almond slices bring an extra crunchiness to the pastry. Once you have tried these you will agree that they are not your average bear claws!

Yield: 9 individual pastries

Ingredients

760 g/1.7 lb croissant dough (page 8)

Almond Filling:

100 g/3.5 oz almond paste

50 g/1.8 oz unsalted butter, at room temperature

1 egg white (about 30 g/1.1 oz)

10 g/0.35 oz (2 tsp) kirsch (cherry brandy)

1 g/0.035 oz (½ tsp) cardamom powder

Zest of one lemon

50 g/1.8 oz almond slices

Baking Finishes:

1 egg

10 g/0.35 oz (2 tsp) heavy cream

Turbinado sugar (raw sugar crystals)

Almond slices

Follow the recipe on page 8 to make a croissant dough. Take one of three portions of the dough (weighs about 760 g/1.7 lb) and cover it with plastic wrap. Reserve the dough in the refrigerator until you are ready to use it.

Almond Filling:

In a mixing bowl, combine the almond paste, butter, egg white, kirsch, cardamom powder, and lemon zest. Mix all the ingredients into a paste using a spoon.

Add the almond slices to the mixture. Mix well. Cover the bowl with plastic wrap. Store the filling in the refrigerator if you are not using it immediately. Use it at room temperature.

Shaping and Baking:

Roll out the croissant dough into a rectangle that is slightly larger than 30-cm x 38-cm/12-in x 15-in in size. Trim off the uneven edges.

Use a knife to cut the dough into three strips, each the size of 30-cm x 13-cm/12-in x 5-in [1].

Place ⅓ of the filling in a row on top of one strip of dough [2]. Brush the bottom edge of the dough with water [3]. Fold the top edge over and adhere it to the bottom edge [4]. Repeat to finish filling the remaining two pieces of dough.

Cut one piece of the filled dough into three equal pieces, each with an approximate size of 10-cm x 6.5-cm/4-in x 2.5-in [5]. For each piece, use a knife to make four 2-cm/0.8-

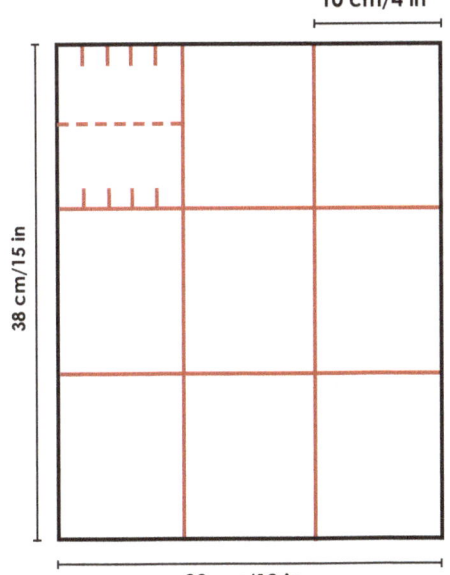

in slits vertically on the bottom edge to form the bear's toes [6]. Bend each piece slightly to separate the toes. Repeat to finish the remaining two strips of dough [7].

Place the shaped bear claws on a baking pan lined with parchment paper while leaving ample space among the pieces. Cover with plastic wrap, and allow the pieces to proof for 1.5 to 2.5 hours or until doubled in volume at room temperature.

Meanwhile, preheat the oven to 188°C/370°F.

In a bowl, whisk the egg with the heavy cream. Brush the pastries gently with the egg wash [8]. Take care not to cover the layers with egg wash. Sprinkle raw sugar crystals and almond slices on top [9].

Bake the pastries for about 20 to 25 minutes until they are golden brown [10]. Let them cool slightly before serving.

THEY BELONG IN A ZOO!

BEAR CLAWS

PIGS IN A BLANKET

PIGS IN A BLANKET

These crispy and flaky pigs in a blanket are filled with sliced ham and Gruyère cheese. Amusingly, they are shaped as a hybrid between a croissant and a pain au chocolat. These pastries are amazingly delicious as a quick meal or snack.

Yield: 8 individual pastries

INGREDIENTS

760 g/1.7 lb croissant dough (page 8)

120 g/4.2 oz Gruyère cheese

160 g/5.6 oz sliced ham

1 egg

10 g/0.35 oz (2 tsp) heavy cream

Follow the recipe on page 8 to make a croissant dough. Take one of three portions of the dough (weighs about 760 g/1.7 lb).

Cut the Gruyère cheese into sticks 8-cm/3.1-in long. Set them aside.

Roll out the croissant dough into a rectangle that is slightly larger than 36-cm x 28-cm/14-in x 11-in in size. Trim off the uneven edges.

Use a knife to mark the dough at 9-cm/3.5-in intervals on the top and bottom edges.

Place a ruler on the dough according to the marks, and cut out a triangular piece that is 9-cm/3.5-in wide at the base and 28-cm/11-in in height. Repeat to cut out the remaining pieces [1].

Take a piece of the dough and place a few slices of ham and one Gruyère cheese stick at the base of the dough piece [2]. Roll up the piece and tug the end underneath the roll itself [3, 4]. Place the roll upright [5]. Finish shaping the remaining pieces.

Place the shaped pastries on a baking pan lined with parchment paper while leaving ample space among the pieces. Cover with plastic wrap, and allow the pieces to proof for 1.5 to 2.5 hours or until doubled in volume at room temperature.

Meanwhile, preheat the oven to 188°C/370°F.

In a bowl, whisk the egg with the heavy cream. Brush the pastries gently with the egg wash [6]. Take care not to cover the layers with egg wash. Bake the pastries for about 20 to 25 minutes until they are golden brown [7, 8]. Let them cool slightly before serving.

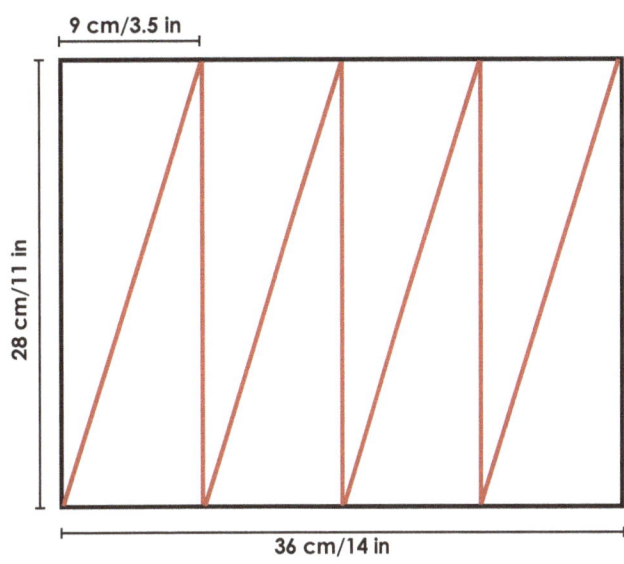

THEY BELONG IN A ZOO! 145

BLUEBERRY MOOSE

A whimsical moose-shaped croissant creation is decorated with blueberry jam and dark chocolate chips. It is pleasing for both the eye and the palate.

Yield: 6 individual pastries

INGREDIENTS

760 g/1.7 lb croissant dough (page 8)

Blueberry Jam:

80 g/2.8 oz granulated sugar

2 g/0.071 oz (½ tsp) powdered pectin

170 g/6 oz blueberry puree

Baking Finishes:

1 egg

10 g/0.35 oz (2 tsp) heavy cream

Dark chocolate chips

Follow the recipe on page 8 to make a croissant dough. Take one of three portions of the dough (weighs about 760 g/1.7 lb) and cover it with plastic wrap. Reserve the dough in the refrigerator until you are ready to use it.

Blueberry Jam:

Combine half of the sugar (40 g/1.4 oz) and the pectin in a mixing bowl. Mix thoroughly and reserve.

In a medium-sized saucepan, combine the blueberry puree with the remaining sugar (40 g/1.4 oz). Bring the mixture to a boil over medium-high heat. Stir in the sugar-pectin mixture [1]. Bring the mixture back to a boil and reduce the heat to medium-low. Stir constantly and cook for another 5 minutes [2].

Let the mixture cool slightly. Cover the surface of the jam with plastic wrap and store the jam in the refrigerator until you are ready to use it.

Shaping and Baking:

Roll out the croissant dough to about 38-cm x 28-cm/15-in x 11-in in size. Use a moose-shaped cutter of 13-cm x 14-cm/5-in x 5.5-in to cut out six pieces of the dough [3].

Place the shaped pastries on a baking pan lined with parchment paper while leaving ample space among the pieces. Cover with plastic wrap, and allow the pieces to proof for 1.5 to 2.5 hours or until doubled in volume at room temperature.

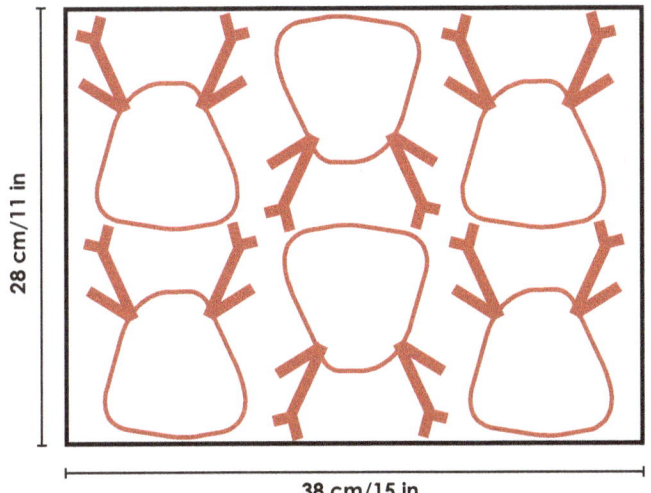

Meanwhile, preheat the oven to 188°C/370°F.

In a bowl, whisk the egg with the heavy cream. Brush the pastries gently with the egg wash. Take care not to cover the layers with egg wash.

Use the back of a round spoon to press the center of each piece [4]. Fill a small pastry bag with the blueberry jam. Pipe a small amount of the jam in the center to resemble a nose [5]. Place two chocolate chips on each piece to resemble eyes [6]. Repeat to finish filling the remaining dough.

Bake the pastries for about 18 to 23 minutes until they are golden brown [7]. Let them cool slightly before serving.

THEY BELONG IN A ZOO!

BLUEBERRY MOOSE

LITTLE PIGS IN A BLANKET

LITTLE PIGS IN A BLANKET

These chubby little treats are absolutely charming! Savory cocktail sausage links are wrapped in wonderfully crispy blankets of croissant dough, shaped like miniature pains au chocolat. They are surely a must-have at any get-together!

Yield: 28 individual pastries

Ingredients

760 g/1.7 lb croissant dough (page 8)

28 cocktail sausage links

1 egg

10 g/0.35 oz (2 tsp) heavy cream

Follow the recipe on page 8 to make a croissant dough. Take one of three portions of the dough (weighs about 760 g/1.7 lb).

Roll out the croissant dough into a rectangle that is slightly larger than 28-cm x 40-cm/11-in x 16-in in size. Trim off the uneven edges.

Use a knife to cut the dough into four strips, each the size of 28-cm x 10-cm/11-in x 4-in [1]. Cut each strip into seven pieces, each the size of 4-cm x 10-cm/1.6-in x 4-in [2]. There will be a total of 28 dough pieces [3].

Take a piece of the dough, and facing the shorter edge, place a sausage link at the bottom horizontally. Roll up the dough to cover the sausage link [4, 5]. Repeat to finish shaping the remaining dough pieces.

Place the shaped pastries on a baking pan lined with parchment paper while leaving ample space among the pieces. Cover with plastic wrap, and allow the pieces to proof for 1.5 to 2.5 hours or until doubled in volume at room temperature.

Meanwhile, preheat the oven to 188°C/370°F.

In a bowl, whisk the egg with the heavy cream. Brush the pastries gently with the egg wash [6]. Take care not to cover the layers with egg wash.

Bake the pastries for about 15 to 18 minutes until they are golden brown [7, 8]. Let them cool slightly before serving.

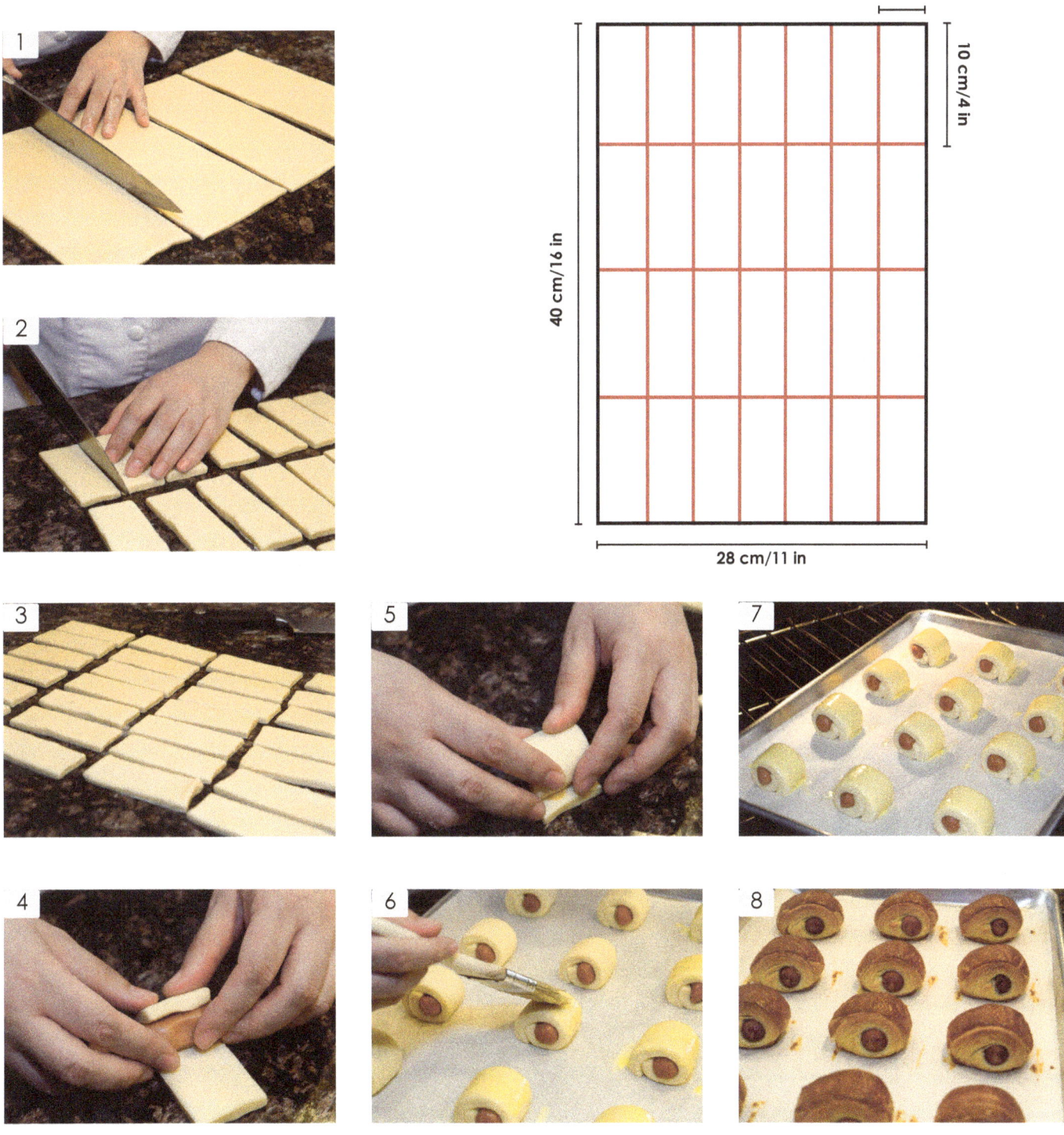

THEY BELONG IN A ZOO!

MONKEY BREAD

Making monkey bread is a clever way to use leftover croissant dough trimmings. The crispy yet moist bite-size dough pieces are covered in cinnamon, sugar, almonds, and raisins. They are the perfect pick-me-ups for tea or coffee!

Yield: 4 mini loaves

INGREDIENTS

530 g/1.2 lb croissant dough trimmings

Almond-Spice Topping:

4 g/0.14 oz (2 tsp) cinnamon powder

100 g/3.5 oz granulated sugar

80 g/2.8 oz raisins

60 g/2.1 oz almond slices

Zest of one lemon

30 g/1.1 oz orange liqueur

Baking Finishes:

Powdered sugar for dusting

After shaping croissant pastries save the leftover dough trimmings.

Almond-Spice Topping:

In a mixing bowl, mix the cinnamon powder and sugar. Set aside.

In another bowl, mix the raisins, almond slices, lemon zest, and orange liqueur. Reserve.

Shaping and Baking:

Cut the dough trimmings into pieces of 2.5-cm/1-in [1]. Toss the dough pieces with the cinnamon-sugar [2].

Place about 70 g/2.5 oz of the cinnamon-sugar-covered dough pieces into a mini paper loaf pan (10-cm x 5-cm x 5-cm/4-in x 2-in x 2-in) [3]. Scatter a layer of raisin-almond mixture on top [4], followed by another layer of dough pieces (about 70 g/2.5 oz). Place a second layer of raisin-almond mixture on top. Repeat to fill the remaining loaf pans. Place the loaf pans on a baking pan lined with parchment paper.

Cover with plastic wrap, and allow the loaves to proof for 1.5 to 2.5 hours or until doubled in volume at room temperature.

Meanwhile, preheat the oven to 188°C/370°F. Bake the pastries for about 25 to 30 minutes until they are golden brown. Dust the tops with powdered sugar [5]. Let them cool slightly before serving.

MONKEY BREAD

BACON MONKEY BREAD

In this savory offering, we use scrap dough left from making regular croissant pastries. It is a simple yet delicious snack, made with smoky bacon and aromatic green onions. After just one bite, you will fall in love with these delicious treats.

Yield: 6 large muffins

INGREDIENTS

500 g/1.1 lb croissant dough trimmings

300 g/11 oz smoked bacon

100 g/3.5 oz chopped green onions

After shaping croissant pastries save the leftover dough trimmings.

In a large sauté pan, cook the bacon strips until most of the fat is rendered. Cook them in batches if necessary.

Let the bacon strips cool completely before continuing. Cut the bacon into small pieces.

Cut the dough trimmings into pieces of 2.5-cm/1-in [1]. Toss the dough pieces with the bacon pieces and chopped green onions [2, 3].

Butter a large muffin pan (6-muffin capacity). Fill each cavity with the bacon-dough mixture [4].

Cover with plastic wrap, and allow the loaves to proof for 1.5 to 2.5 hours or until doubled in volume at room temperature.

Meanwhile, preheat the oven to 188°C/370°F.

Bake the pastries for about 20 to 25 minutes until they are golden brown [5]. Unmold them from the muffin pan. Let them cool slightly before serving.

BACON MONKEY BREAD

ALSO AVAILABLE

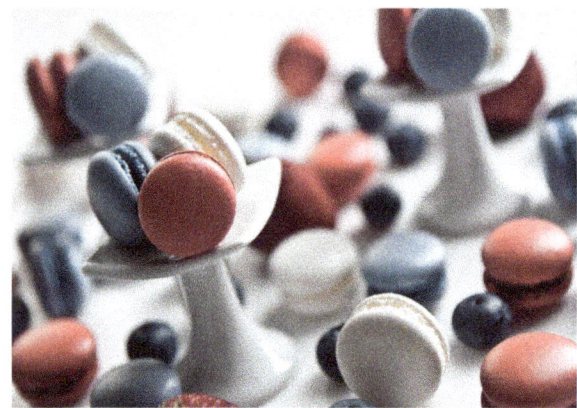

MACARON MAGIC
Jialin Tian, Ph.D.
Photographs & Design by Jialin Tian
Step-by-Step Photographs by Yabin Yu

MACARON MAGIC 2
Individual Desserts and Showpieces
Jialin Tian, Ph.D.
Photographs & Design by Jialin Tian
Step-by-Step Photographs by Yabin Yu

CHOUX TEMPTATIONS
Jialin Tian, Ph.D.
Photographs & Design by Jialin Tian
Step-by-Step Photographs by Yabin Yu

Little Choux Temptations
Jialin Tian, Ph.D.
Photographs & Design by Jialin Tian
Step-by-Step Photographs by Yabin Yu

COMING SOON

www.ingramcontent.com/pod-product-compliance
Lightning Source LLC
Chambersburg PA
CBHW040042100526
44583CB00027BA/3258